30
Meditations
on
REST

30
Meditations
on
REST

Marilyn Hickey
& Sarah Bowling

WHITAKER
HOUSE

30 MEDITATIONS ON REST
Marilyn Hickey Ministries
P.O. Box 6598
Englewood, CO 80155
www.marilynandsarah.org

ISBN: 978-1-60374-901-5
eBook ISBN: 978-1-60374-902-2
Printed in the United States of America
© 2013 by Marilyn Hickey Ministries

Whitaker House
1030 Hunt Valley Circle
New Kensington, PA 15068
www.whitakerhouse.com

Library of Congress Cataloging-in-Publication Data (Pending)

FOREWORD

In the twenty-first century, meditation has become a lost spiritual discipline.

During the time of Christ, some rabbinic schools required students to memorize the entire Torah, or at least the Pentateuch. In the Middle Ages, individuals memorized the entire book of Psalms. Jesus overcame temptation through memorized Scripture. The apostles quoted Scripture in their sermons and in their writings.

Today, many followers of Christ have electronic versions of the Bible loaded onto their phones, their iPads, and their computers, as well as dust-covered physical Bibles, stacked on bookshelves; but few followers of Christ systematically meditate upon the Word of God.

Marilyn Hickey has personally inspired me to meditate on the Word of God. I know her teachings will inspire you, too.

—*Dr. Darryl Wootton*
Lead Pastor, First Assembly of God
Bartlesville, Oklahoma

CONTENTS

INTRODUCTION

MEDITATING: THE #1 KEY TO SUCCESS

Hide-and-seek was a fun game. I can hear the refrain: "Ready or not, here I come!" One child was "it," and he would cover his eyes on home base as all the other children ran and hid. The object was for those who were hiding to get "home" before they were found.

It was great entertainment, and amusing, but there's a "hiding" that is essential to our walk as Christians that I want to present here.

I'm referring to hiding the Word in our hearts, and the "who, what, when, where, and how" of doing this. The Bible says, "*Your word I have hidden in my heart, that I might not sin against You!*" (Psalm 119:11). When we hide the Word in our hearts, it not only keeps us from sin, as the psalmist said, but it also will bring success.

Most promises in the Bible relate to specific actions:

"Honor your father and mother," which is the first command-
ment with promise: "that it may be well with you and you may
live long on the earth."   (Ephesians 6:2–3)

The command (action) involves honoring your parents, and it
is accompanied by a specific promise: that you may be well and
"live long on the earth."

God gave a command to Joshua. It was given because of God's
promise to lead Israel into the Promised Land. After forty years in
the wilderness, Joshua was chosen to fulfill the hundreds-of-years-
old pledge. In Joshua 1:8, he received a command to meditate. The
instruction was for *all people*, as you'll see from reading further
Scriptures on meditation, and it carries a promise that goes with
everything in your life. This Scripture enlightens us about hiding
the Word. It says,

This Book of the Law shall not depart from your mouth, but
you shall meditate in it day and night, that you may observe to
do according to all that is written in it. For then you will make
your way prosperous, and then you will have good success.
                                              (Joshua 1:8)

God said, in effect, "If you meditate on My Word, day and
night, and if you speak that Word and obey it, everything in your
life will be prosperous and successful!"

I've discovered that God has a lot to say about meditating, and
I've become excited about what meditating on His Word accom-
plishes. It is important that you understand what meditation is
and what it will do for you. Meditating on God's Word changes
lives—in fact, it *is* life.

I've heard many testimonies regarding the effects of medica-
tion. If you know me, I'm sure most of you know Sarah Bowling.
She's a wife, a mother, a teacher of the Word, a pastor, and my

television cohost on *Today with Marilyn and Sarah*. And, if you did not know, she is my daughter. She ministers alongside Reece Bowling, her husband, who is senior pastor of Orchard Road Christian Center, in Greenwood, Colorado. The crux of her heart's cry is a ministry she founded, called Saving Moses, which concentrates on saving young children, from newborns to the age of five.

Sarah's life has been strongly affected by meditation. This is what she says:

> The most powerful experience I've had meditating on the Bible was when I was in my early twenties. I was spending the summer doing missions work in Hong Kong. At the time, I was a schoolteacher and had made some bad decisions in my personal life during the preceding school year. During my time there, I was not only involved in missions work but I also was trying to get past the dilemma created by those choices. Thankfully, I had supportive people around me and made great friendships.

> Over the course of that summer, what helped my thinking the most was my experience with memorizing and meditating on Colossians 3. I found that the longer I memorized and meditated on those verses, the more healthy my mind and thoughts became. As I continued to progress through the chapter, it felt as though the verses I memorized were figuratively washing out all the garbage those bad decisions had deposited in my mind. Furthermore, it felt like those verses were not only cleaning my mind, but they also were replacing destructive mind-sets with more truth-oriented thoughts and convictions.

> I've never forgotten that experience and the transforming power of meditating on the Bible. Subsequently, I've

used the principles of meditating over the course of my life with equally powerful results and transformations.

I'm sure most of you are familiar with Rick Warren's book, *The Purpose Driven Life*. Rick is the founder and senior pastor of Saddleback Church, in Forest Lake, California. This is what he said in his book about meditation:

> Meditation is "thinking about God"—His essence, His desires, His plans, His mercy, etc.—throughout each day. And the only way a Christian can do this is by knowing God—and the only way a Christian can know God is through His Word. Meditation (similar to the process of "worrying"), which is only "focused thinking," is accomplished when one mulls over (contemplates, ponders) God's Word continually during the day.
>
> Meditation allows God to share His secrets (revelations) with His children—to speak to His children in a close and personal way. To properly meditate requires a life of studying God's thoughts recorded in the Bible. It also means that a Christian should continuously review biblical truths when they are presented in sermons, radio broadcasts, Bible studies, etc."[1]

Meditation isn't always easy, and it's no small wonder the enemy has desperately tried to mask the topic of meditation on God's Word. He's brought in many counterfeits, such as transcendental meditation, and all kinds of distraction. Whenever you see the devil putting up a smokescreen, you can be sure he's counterfeiting something real. The devil never created anything. All he can do is falsify and imitate what already exists.

---

1. Rick Warren, *The Purpose Driven Life* (Grand Rapids, MI: Zondervan, 2002), 85.

1

THE "WHO" OF MEDITATION

I mentioned earlier God's promise for success in Joshua 1:8.

What is success? Let's look at the Hebrew word for *"prosperous"*: *tsalach*.

It means:

1. to rush

2. to advance, prosper, make progress, succeed, be profitable

3. to make prosperous, bring to successful issue, cause to prosper

4. to show or experience prosperity, prosper

You see how success and prosperity go hand in hand? This Hebrew word has the correct signification. When I read "to advance," I think of wading across a river or pushing forward toward a goal. Proverbs 13:19 says, *"A desire accomplished is sweet to the soul."*

Another meaning of this word is "to fall upon." Picture God's riches falling upon you. Also hidden in this good word is the meaning "to finish well." God's Word has happy endings.

Lastly, it can be translated as "promote." The Hebrew connotation means it brings promotion.

If you so desired, you could place meditate before each meaning and make an equation straight across the line. Do you want to prosper as a wife, a husband, a mother, an employer, an employee, a friend, a sweetheart, a neighbor, a minister, or as a Christian? Meditation on God's Word is the unusual key that unlocks all of His success. It is the solution, and we need to know what it is and how to do it.

Many will say that this passage was only written for Joshua. They may say, "Well, God gave Joshua success because he had to take the Promised Land." But I want to tell you that God did more than tell us to take the Promised Land—He told us to take the world for Jesus.

Meditation can dramatically change your life. In this passage, God is talking about a "blessed man." He says:

> *Blessed is the man who walks not in the counsel of the ungodly, nor stands in the path of sinners, nor sits in the seat of the scornful; but his delight is in the law of the LORD, and in His law he meditates day and night. He shall be like a tree planted by the rivers of water, that brings forth its fruit in its season, whose leaf also shall not wither; and whatever he does shall prosper.* (Psalm 1:1–3)

If you meditate on the Word day and night, you'll implement the key element of being blessed, prosperous, and successful in every area of your life.

"Oh," you say, "there's that ugly word *meditate*." I think some Christians have this word confused with *medicate*. I think they associate it with a task that is time-consuming and difficult. However, meditation does not need to be drudgery. Rather, I have discovered that it adds a *refreshing* quality to my study of God's

Word. It is my desire for you to see transformation take place when you begin applying the principles of meditation to your own life. As Rick Warren suggested, if you know how to worry, you already know how to meditate!

In the passage above, we run into the same idea found in Joshua 1:8. *"Blessed is the man...."* The man who meditated on the Word will be prosperous and successful in all that he does. Shall we embrace the truth of meditating? Or shall we simply stand aside and, with words and acts, watch other Christians meditate? We are too busy, too old, or too "out of it" to be bothered.

However, you see, Psalm 1 whets every believer's appetite for meditation. It states, *"Blessed is the man who...meditates"* (Psalm 1:1–2). The word *blessedness* is not found in the Hebrew text, because there is no such thing as a singular blessing, only plural blessings. Psalm 1 says that meditating will give you vitality *"like a tree"* (Psalm 1:3). It will give you security, for you will be *"planted"* (verse 3). Your capacity will be unlimited because His sources are *"the rivers* [plural] *of water"* (verse 3). You will be fertile, because meditating *"brings forth its fruit"* (verse 3). You will have seasons and perpetuate, because your *"leaf...shall not wither"* (verse 3). What prosperity! Everything you do *"shall prosper"* (verse 3).

Can you look into the mirror of these words and see yourself?

Because of the blessings, successes, and revelations I've received, I've condensed hours of study, practical experience, and character studies on meditation, which I believe will compel you to meditate on His Word—letting it dominate and change your life for the better. I pray the Lord will throw open the shutters of your spiritual understanding so that you may receive all the blessings He has for you in the fullness of His Word.

Let this truth be gladly received in your mind and your will. Embrace this truth. There's only one way to go—forward!

2

THE "WHAT" OF MEDITATION

*"This Book of the Law shall not depart from your mouth, but
you shall meditate in it day and night, that you may observe to
do according to all that is written in it. For then you will make
your way prosperous, and then you will have good success."*
—Joshua 1:8

Meditate—a word abused, misused, and charged by Christians
as an unscriptural principle. Yet God spoke to Joshua, saying that
if he would not allow His Word to depart out of his mouth, but
instead meditate on it day and night, observing to do it, He would
make everything Joshua put his hands to prosper and be successful. It's a simple thing for us to rationalize and simply pass off the
strong admonition given to Joshua. It's easy to insist that the command was for Joshua only. After all, he had a big Promised Land
to conquer. However, lest we speak too lightly of such words, Jesus
told us to conquer a gigantic world with His Word. If meditation on the Word conquered Canaan, a land of giants, as well as
walled cities, and brought forth milk and honey, could it conquer

our giants, bring down the walls of our opposition, and pour forth milk and honey into our daily lives? Could we, too, conquer a world of Canaanites, as Joshua did?

What is meditation? It is to chew, to mutter, to memorize, visualize, and personalize the Word of God. Meditation presents a zealous promise that is tremendous in scope.

Genesis 24:63 is the first reference to meditation recorded in the Bible: "*And Isaac went out to meditate in the field in the evening; and he lifted his eyes and looked, and there, the camels were coming.*"

It was the first time Isaac laid eyes on his beloved Rebekah, and it was love at first sight. And it happened as he was meditating.

What can we glean from this initial reference? It says, Isaac "*lifted his eyes.*" I've found lifting your eyes will help you to see Jesus in your circumstances. When Abraham "*lifted his eyes,*" he received a divine visitation. He also "*lifted his eyes*" (Genesis 22:13) when Isaac was delivered from being sacrificed on Mount Moriah.

God's promises were incubated with Abram (who later became Abraham). He spoke to Abram the first time and told him to do three things:

1. Leave the city of Ur.

2. Don't take relatives.

3. Go to the Promised Land.

God told Abram he would receive specific blessings for obeying. When he fully obeyed these three commands, he received the blessings (promises) the Lord set forth. Even though he didn't see them all come about in his lifetime, he received them nonetheless.

As we know, Abraham wanted Isaac to have a righteous wife. He didn't want him to marry any Canaanite women. We'll see why later. So, he called for his servant, who took a vow to find the right woman. He found Rebekah and brought her to meet Isaac.

As we read, the Bible tells us that Isaac was meditating in the field. Now this happened at night, mind you, when one wouldn't anticipate anyone coming to his home. Isaac lifted his eyes. What caused him to do this? It was dark, and he probably couldn't see very well. Don't you think his meditation had something to do with it?

The Hebrew word used here for *meditation* is used only once in the Bible: *suwach.* It means "to muse," which is to ponder, consider, or mull over. So here we have Isaac, at the end of the day, in the field by himself. What a lonely portrait. However, he was most likely ruminating on the promises God gave to his father, Abraham. God's pledge to him was,

I will make you a great nation; I will bless you and make your name great; and you shall be a blessing. I will bless those who bless you, and I will curse him who curses you; and in you all the families of the earth shall be blessed.

(Genesis 12:2–3)

These promises included assurances of another land, another nation, and a spiritual blessing for generations to come. They were great and mighty promises, and they required that Isaac marry the right woman. No doubt, it weighed heavy on his shoulders as he deliberated. That evening, his answer came; God solved his dilemma.

How is that going to help you? Lift up your eyes. The Lord knows the perfect one for you. You don't. Maybe you're already married, and you don't need a mate. Lift up your eyes and thank God for the mate you have. But know that as you meditate on His promises, He will bring them to pass. I love how God works.

To meditate gives forth the flavorful meaning of being separated, as the dross is separated from the silver. So, must a man separate himself from the crowd in order to help the crowd? Isn't that goofy? Proverbs 25:4 says, *"Take away the dross from the silver, and there shall come forth a vessel for the finer"* (KJV).

Psalm 119:15 says, *"I will meditate on Your precepts, and contemplate Your ways."* It gives the idea of bowing down and musing. There is the idea of a pilgrimage in this word. Imagine, taking a trip into God's Word. Fantastic!

Lastly is the concept of Psalm 39:3, *"My heart was hot within me; while I was musing, the fire burned. Then I spoke with my tongue."* It infers the focusing of the rays of God's love and power on a man's heart, which starts a fire, before the tongue begins to speak. This sums up the process of taking the Word, speaking it, walking with it, and allowing it to guide you.

Bill Gothard has stated that meditating is: (1) to memorize, (2) to personalize, and (3) to spiritualize. How precise and true.

As you see, to meditate is to walk and talk. Plan on becoming a spiritual "walkie-talkie."

Scriptures on meditation say that if you meditate on the Word, keeping it in your mind, letting it go from there to your mouth, and acting on it, you will be successful spiritually, physically, mentally, and emotionally. As a parent, a spouse, a child, a cook, or a student—no matter what you do—you will be prosperous if you obey the command in Joshua 1:8. This is a Scripture key in the Bible that carries tremendous impact.

Three Components of Joshua 1:8

As we continue to look at what meditation is, we see three parts to Joshua 1:8.

Part one involves your mouth: *"This Book of the Law shall not depart from your mouth."*

The Message version reads, "*And don't for a minute let this Book of The Revelation be out of mind.*"

You have to spend time thinking the Word first, which, of course, comes by reading. Please realize that as you memorize a Scripture, it is for you. Visualize it in your mind's eye. Part two involves the meditation itself: "*You shall meditate in it day and night.*" I mentioned *to mutter* earlier. The Hebrew word *meditate* translates as "to moan, growl, utter, muse, mutter, meditate, devise, plot, and speak." Remember that meditation involves "talking" God's Word, or muttering. By doing this, you will fulfill the first part of this command, and then you will not let it depart from your mouth. You may say, "Wait a minute. You're telling me to speak, but also that it won't depart from my mouth." Yes, when you mutter the word and speak it to yourself, it will become ingrained in your brain, rooted in your mind. It won't depart from you, I promise.

Part three brings in the action: "*...that you may observe to do according to all that is written in it.*" Meditation not only involves thinking and talking, but it also involves walking. We are to be doers of God's Word, not hearers only. (See James 1:22.)

These three elements of meditation bring forth the promise, "*...then you will make your way prosperous, and then you will have good success.*"

Many people say, "If only there was something that I could do about this terrible situation." What can you do? Meditate on the Word.

God did not say, "If you'll do this, I'll make your way prosperous." He said, in effect, "If you'll meditate, *you* will make your way prosperous." That is a big difference. You alone are the deciding factor. God will never force you to meditate on His Word; neither will He force prosperity on you. Meditation on God's Word is a consuming effort, not merely a pastime.

The word *meditate* in the above Scripture means to speak with oneself in a low voice, or to think aloud on the Word of God. This keeps the mind saturated with God's truth so that it can give a proper answer.

Joshua Affected Three Ways

There's something interesting about the first chapter of the book of Joshua. There are three separate places in the chapter where God told Joshua to be strong and courageous.

The first instance is in Joshua 1:6:

Be strong and of good courage, for to this people you shall divide as an inheritance the land which I swore to their fathers to give them.

This command appears in two other places:

Only be strong and very courageous, that you may observe to do according to all the law which Moses My servant commanded you; do not turn from it to the right hand or to the left, that you may prosper wherever you go. (verse 7)

Have I not commanded you? Be strong and of good courage; do not be afraid, nor be dismayed, for the LORD your God is with you wherever you go. (verse 9)

That bothered me at first. I wondered, *Why did God tell Joshua to be strong and courageous three times in the same chapter that He tells Joshua to meditate on the Word?* Then I looked carefully at those verses, and I realized that God wanted Joshua to be strong and courageous in three different ways:

　　1. In his body

2. In his spirit

3. In his soul (his mind, emotions, and will)

First, let's see how God wanted to strengthen Joshua physically. When the Lord told him to capture the Promised Land for his people, Joshua was more than eighty years old. He was going to need supernatural strength to take that land. And he received strength in his body; and you will, too.

Then, in Joshua 1:7, the Lord spoke about Joshua's spirit. He said, *"Do not turn from it to the right hand or to the left."* Just stay with it, and receive it into your spirit. Joshua received strength and courage in his spirit. This Scripture pertains to all of us.

Finally, God spoke to Joshua about having strength and courage in his soul when he said, *"Do not be afraid, nor be dismayed"* (Joshua 1:9). God wanted to bind Joshua with the wonderful strength provided through His Word in every area of his life. Joshua received strength through meditation, and so can you.

A Foundation

Since God told Joshua that meditation on the Word would make him prosperous and successful, I decided to study Joshua's life, and I saw that the "proof of the pudding is in the eating." After examining his life, I discovered that meditation had a definite impact on all that Joshua did. Before we look at how this occurred, I want you to understand what is involved.

Changes in Your Life

Are there areas in your life that need changed or a refreshed? The Bible says if you meditate on the Word of God day and night, you'll be prosperous and successful in every area of your life. The

Word profited my very first meditation partner in the area of her personality, because she considered the Word, instead of her problems. It was tremendous to see the transformation that occurred in her life. I want to challenge you to meditate on the Word of God and see how it will change your life, too. Meditation isn't just for Joshua, and it isn't just for pastors—it's for you, too!

Three Basic Steps

The three basic steps of meditation are:

1. Memorize
2. Personalize
3. Visualize

Memorize

If you're like most people, you may get uptight as soon as you hear the word *memorize*. Some people say, "I'm beyond forty years old; I can't memorize anymore." Don't say that. The Bible says you have the mind of Christ. (See 1 Corinthians 2:16.) In John 14:26, Jesus promised, *"But the Helper, the Holy Spirit, whom the Father will send in My name, He will teach you all things, and bring to your remembrance all things that I said to you."* This is very important: How can the Holy Spirit bring something to your remembrance if there is nothing to remember? You are to meditate God's Word so that He can make you remember.

Personalize

As you meditate, don't just say, "This is God's Word to all Christians." You should say, "This is God's Word for *me*!" Some people read the Bible as though it's for everybody but them. God isn't a respecter of persons. (See Acts 10:34 kjv.) That means that He is not more interested in other people. His promises are for you.

Visualize

You must see God's Word as finished. See His Word happening in your life, in spite of what your circumstances may look like. I call visualization "faith sight." Visualization is found in the life of Abraham:

> *By faith Abraham, when he was tested, offered up Isaac, and he who had received the promises offered up his only begotten son, of whom it was said, "In Isaac your seed shall be called," concluding that God was able to raise him up, even from the dead, from which he also received him in a figurative sense.*
> (Hebrews 11:17–19)

When Abraham was on his way to offer Isaac to the Lord as a sacrifice of consecration, he told his servants, *"Stay here with the donkey; the lad and I will go yonder and worship, and we will come back to you"* (Genesis 22:5). What was Abraham saying? He was visualizing God's promise to bless his seed—Isaac, his son. He was seeing God's Word as complete truth, and saying, in effect, "Even if I do sacrifice Isaac and God has to resurrect him from the ashes, He has made me a promise, and He will keep it." Abraham was seeing God's Word as complete, through visualization, which caused him to receive Isaac "in a figure."

When you meditate on the Word, begin saying what God says; accept His Word as a reality in your life; visualize it happening.

Have you ever daydreamed? Everybody has. You can have a spiritual dream by visualizing God's Word as if it were already accomplished in your life. This is the final step involved in the threefold process of meditation: first, you memorize; second, you personalize; and third, you visualize the results.

Joshua's Life of Meditation

Joshua's life was a testimony of the power of meditation and the blessings that it brings. Even in his mistakes, he was still prosperous and successful.

One of his mistakes was allowing himself to be deceived by some Gibeonite people. Gibeonites came from the Hivite tribe. *Hivite* means "snake" or "serpent." The Gibeonites were living in the land where the children of Israel were. It's easy to see why Hivite means "snake," because these people were crafty.

> *But when the inhabitants of Gibeon heard what Joshua had done to Jericho and Ai, they worked craftily, and went and pretended to be ambassadors. And they took old sacks on their donkeys, old wineskins torn and mended, old and patched sandals on their feet, and old garments on themselves; and all the bread of their provision was dry and moldy. And they went to Joshua, to the camp at Gilgal, and said to him and to the men of Israel, "We have come from a far country; now therefore, make a covenant with us."* (Joshua 9:3–6)

God distinctly warned Joshua not to make a covenant with the Gibeonites; but when they came to him, he didn't realize who they were, and he entered into a covenant with them.

> *They said to Joshua, "We are your servants." And Joshua said to them, "Who are you, and where do you come from?" So they said to him: "From a very far country your servants have come, because of the name of the Lord your God; for we have heard of His fame, and all that He did in Egypt, and all that He did to the two kings of the Amorites who were beyond the Jordan; to Sihon king of Heshbon, and Og king of Bashan, who was at Ashtaroth."* (Joshua 9:8–10)

The Gibeonites were intimidated by the Israelites, having heard about their victories in past battles. They wanted to be assured of favor and protection, which they would be guaranteed through a covenant.

Joshua made a covenant with them, and three days later, he received news that made him angry:

> And it happened at the end of three days, after they had made a covenant with them, that they heard that they were their neighbors who dwelt near them.   (Joshua 9:16)

Now what would Joshua do? This did not look like a prosperous situation. The people said, "We have sworn to them by the LORD God of Israel; now therefore, we may not touch them" (Joshua 9:19). The Lord knew Joshua was a man of the Word. He had caused the Gibeonites to be their servants, and their descendants were a group of people called the Nethinims, meaning "devoted men of God."

After the children of Israel made a league with the Gibeonites, a king of Jerusalem heard about the victories that the Lord had given the Israelites. He also heard that the Israelites had covenanted with the Gibeonites, and, because Gibeon was a great city, he felt threatened. He sent armies to make war against Gibeon, but the men of camp called on Joshua:

> Do not forsake your servants; come up to us quickly, save us and help us, for all the kings of the Amorites who dwell in the mountains have gathered together against us. (Joshua 10:6)

What happened? God protected the Israelites and their servants. First, He sent hail that only hit the attacking army. Then, He sent confusion and ambush, which caused them to fight against each other. And something else happened that made this day unique to its kind:

Then Joshua spoke to the LORD...*and he said in the sight of Israel: "Sun, stand still over Gibeon; and moon, in the Valley of Aijalon." So the sun stood still, and the moon stopped, till the people had revenge upon their enemies.*

(Joshua 10:12–13)

When Joshua spoke, even the sun and the moon stood still. Here is a man who kept God's powerful Word in his mouth all the time. Joshua meditated on the Word and moved in its authority.

Do you need the power and strength of God in your life? Do you want to be prosperous? The key is meditation.

Then I wondered, *What about Joshua's financial statement? He was successful physically, because he led the Israelites to take the Promised Land, and it only took them six-and-a-half years to take it. Was Joshua financially successful?*

Many people imagine the children of Israel to be dressed in rags, owning next to nothing, as they wandered through the land. That is not so. When the Israelites cast lots to determine where people would settle, according to their tribes, Joshua did not choose some little old tent. No. He asked for the city Timnath Serah (see Joshua 19:50), which means "the city of the sun." Joshua owned a whole mountain with a city on top of it. Some would say, "I'm going to be humble; just give me a little nest in the west." Joshua received a double portion of wealth. Why? Because his priority was the Word of God.

If you are in the ministry, there are those who may wonder about your family. Once, when I was teaching in a church, a big, tall, Church-of-God minister stood up, turned to me and said, "I'd like to ask you, what does your husband think about you traveling all over the countryside?" I thought, *Oh, God, give me a good answer.* Then I asked him, "Which husband?" Everybody laughed, and that night, he came forward after the service and received the baptism of the Holy Spirit. People always wonder about your family when you're in the ministry, and I wondered the same thing about Joshua's family. The Lord showed me the answer, too. It's in Joshua 24:15–16:

> [Joshua said,] *"But as for me and my house, we will serve the* LORD." *So the people answered and said: "Far be it from us that we should forsake the* LORD *to serve other gods."*

Joshua and his family served the Lord. And what happened? They inspired all of the people of Israel to serve the Lord, too. A family that diligently seeks after God will bring Him glory, and meditating on God's Word will bring you total success in your family life.

Sometimes in my own life, when situations have appeared impossible, I've reminded the Lord, "You said that if I meditated on Your Word day and night, my way would be prosperous and successful. That includes my children."

Meanings of *Meditate*

The word *meditate* is translated from three Hebrew words and two Greek words. One of the Hebrew words, *hagah,* found in both Joshua 1:8 and Psalm 1:2, means "to speak to one's self in a low voice," "to think out loud the Word of God," and "to keep the mind saturated with truth for a proper answer." *Meditate* can also mean "to separate the dross from the silver," as used in Proverbs 25:4: *"Take away the dross from the silver, and there shall come forth a vessel for the finer."*

Why separate the dross from the silver? To purify it. Meditation brings forth a cleansing; it is the washing of the water of the Word. How does a silversmith know that the silver is pure when he separates it from the dross? Because he can see his image reflected in it. Meditating on the Word of God will cleanse and purify you, so that His image will be reflected in all that you do. Your personality will be more like His than ever before, and you will be prosperous and successful in all that you do. You'll be "*a vessel for the finer.*"

There's a beautiful picture formed by the Hebrew word *hagah*. The first letter, as it's written in Hebrew, is He, which stands for grace. The second is Gimel, which means "camel," and the third is He again. The depiction we see is grace, a camel to travel, and another level of grace. You may say that God gives us the means (the camel) to travel from grace to grace. Remember Genesis 24:63, when Isaac was meditating in the field in the evening? He lifted his eyes and, behold, camels were coming.

Just as Isaac bowed in reverence to the Lord, you, too, can literally bow in holy reverence to Him as you meditate; this is a precious practice. If you are meditating in a place where bowing is impossible, I believe you can "bow in your spirit" unto Him. It is a state of giving Him total control, when your mind, spirit, and body are subject to the Lord.

In this verse of Scripture, Isaac bowed and mused over God's Word. As I said earlier, when he lifted his eyes, camels approached, bringing him his bride. How wonderful it must have been: The first time Rebekah ever saw her husband, he was meditating on the Word of God.

Also recall Psalm 39:3, which offers another concept of meditation: "*My heart was hot within me; while I was musing, the fire burned. Then I spoke with my tongue.*" The word *muse* means to meditate, and it focuses on God's love and power, starting a fire in a man's heart, causing him to speak. Jeremiah once refused to speak the Word of God, but then he said, "*But His word was in my heart like a burning fire shut up in my bones; I was weary of holding it back, and I could not*" (Jeremiah 20:9).

In Luke 24:32, the disciples saw Jesus after His ascension, and they said, *"Did not our heart burn within us while He talked with us on the road, and while He opened the Scriptures to us?"*

The Word of God will start a spiritual fire within you, and then it will cause you to utter words and articulate sounds with your voice. Meditate on the Word of God, let it come out as fire, burning the chaff out of your life.

Meditating is supremely the most important thing that you, as a Christian, can do.

3

THE "WHEN" OF MEDITATION

Meditation carries the highest level of importance. The following Scripture provides a key for *when* we should meditate:

> *My son, keep your father's command, and do not forsake the law of your mother. Bind them continually upon your heart; tie them around your neck. When you roam, they will lead you; when you sleep, they will keep you; and when you awake, they will speak with you.* (Proverbs 6:20–22)

I memorize Scripture first thing in the morning, even before I brush my teeth. It's the best time, because my mind is clear and fresh. I recall my Scriptures early in the afternoon, because God's Word guides me. Then, the last thing I do before I go to sleep is say my Scriptures for the day aloud once again. You'll read more about this in chapter 5—the "How" section.

That final time I speak the Scripture, it saturates my very being. Solomon spoke these words to his people: *"Let your heart therefore be loyal to the LORD our God, to walk in His statutes and keep His commandments, as at this day"* (1 Kings 8:61). You say this takes discipline. You are so right. Isn't discipline worth it when it makes you prosperous and successful in all you do?

One night, a woman broke into our house when I was there alone. Actually, our toy poodle was with me, but that wasn't going to be of much help. However, God delivered me.

Several passages in the Bible talk about deliverance from evil by the blood of Jesus. (See Hebrews 2:14; Colossians 1:13; 2:15; 1 John 3:8; Revelation 12:11.) I had memorized this verse: "*He has delivered us from the power of darkness and conveyed us into the kingdom of the Son of His love*" (Colossians 1:13). I spoke this Word and found that it kept me; and I was delivered, praise be to God.

There are days when Scripture memorization goes easily and every taste of His Word in my mouth is delicious. But then there are days when it's hard; it feels drab and discouraging. There are times of tremendous pressure on my time and energy, and there are times when my mind is fuzzy with exhaustion. There are also times when the enemy whispers, *What is this proving?* However, beyond all of this is, "the entrance of His Word gives light" (see Psalm 119:130)—a light I've never known before.

Job stored the Word, and it became gold in his heart:

> *Receive, please, instruction from His mouth, and lay up His words in your heart. If you return to the Almighty, you will be built up; you will remove iniquity far from your tents. Then you will lay your gold in the dust, and the gold of Ophir among the stones of the brooks.* (Job 22:22–24)

David said, "*My soul shall be satisfied as with marrow and fatness, and my mouth shall praise You with joyful lips. When I remember You on my bed, I meditate on You in the night watches*" (Psalm 63:5–6). He found that meditating at night brought richness to his soul. His meditation brought him through tremendous trials.

I once spoke with a lovely pastor's wife in Rapid City, South Dakota, and she told me, "I have started an 'M&M Club' in our church; it means *Memorize* and *Meditate*." She said, "There are sixteen of us that meet once a week, and we have memory partners. We get together to encourage each other with revelations that we've received during the week." She shared a lot of things about meditation with me that God had revealed to me, too. She spoke of how the Word of God had literally transformed them.

Meditating takes the Word and makes it glow within you; it puts fire in your mouth. It will put lightness in your steps and brightness in your eyes. The saturating of your spirit in the Word will conquer old problems and make new victories a reality. I've yet to meet one person who was sorry they memorized and meditated on the Word of God. You won't be sorry either.

Key Moments

One time, I took a private plane to a seminar in Billings, Montana. We departed early in the morning and decided to return home late that night. That evening, the plane would not start. The pilot said, "Oh, it's the battery." Someone was sent to recharge it, but when the plane finally rolled down the runway, one of the women onboard said, "The wheel on my side is on fire."

I looked out the window on my side and confirmed that the wheel was indeed on fire, and I told the pilot.

"Oh," the pilot responded, "the wheels aren't on fire; the brakes are."

"Isn't that dangerous?"

"No," he said. "We've just recharged the battery, and we're going against the wind. We'll taxi around, and the fire will go out."

The pilot was calm, but I didn't feel very peaceful. Neither did the woman beside me. She said, "I think you should suggest that we stay in Billings tonight."

Trying to remain tactful, I said to the pilot, "Roger, do you think that it's safe for us to leave Billings tonight?"

"Don't you think that I know how to fly this plane?" he asked. "If I didn't think this was safe, I wouldn't be doing it."

I told the woman next to me, "Virginia, you ask the next time." Then, I said, "Let's pray that, if God doesn't want us to leave Billings tonight, He'll cause the plane to be unable to take off." We prayed.

I don't know how far we were from Billings when the pilot lifted the plane's wheels, but when he did, every light and electrical instrument in that plane went out. My only thought was, *The electricity took up the wheels, and we have no electricity to put them back down.* I'd never been in a plane that landed without wheels, and I really did not want to be in one. I was frightened.

The pilot asked, "Does anybody have a flashlight?"

I thought, *Who carries a flashlight around?* That's not something that I normally carry during my travels. Nobody had one. The pilot could not see the dials, and with the radio dead, he could not call in. It was raining, so there was no depth or speed perception at all. Then I heard the pilot say, "We'd better prepare for a crash landing."

At that moment, a thought struck me: *The Word will keep me.* The Lord brought to mind this precious Scripture:

> *"No weapon formed against you shall prosper, and every tongue which rises against you in judgment You shall condemn. This is the heritage of the servants of the LORD, and their righteousness is from Me," says the LORD.* (Isaiah 54:17)

You will find that when you meditate on the Word of God, He will bring Scriptures to your mind at key moments in your life. Some Scriptures that I memorize will not return to me until ten weeks later, but I've discovered that the Lord will bring them back when I really need them. He gave me that Scripture on the plane when I surely needed it.

"Behold, You desire truth in the inward parts, and in the hidden part You will make me to know wisdom" (Psalm 51:6). Truth is the Word of God. I had put truth into my spirit, and God activated it in my life, making it wisdom. If there had been nothing there to "activate," there wouldn't have been any wisdom; but that night in the plane, God's Word became wisdom and vibrant life to me.

I repeated the Scripture aloud. I said it again. What happened? The plane turned around and we landed in Billings without a problem. I saw the Word of God work with power that night.

Do you want the Word of God to work tangibly in your life? Do you want it to make you prosperous in every area of your life? Meditation is your key. Unless you commit yourself to God's answers, you cannot expect His results. You'll find His answer to whatever you need by meditating upon His Word.

4

THE "WHERE" OF MEDITATION

One of the best things about the Bible is that it provides us with practical examples, and these examples are evidence that God's Word works. I want you to see the importance of meditation and where it has been used. As we've seen, Joshua 1:8 proclaims that the key to all prosperity and success is not to let the Word depart out of your mouth, but to meditate on it, day and night, doing what it says. In fact, the history of the children of Israel is enveloped in meditation.

We tend to associate certain people with Scripture, by saying, "It is their ministry to study the Word." God didn't say studying the Word was a priority only for those in the ministry. He desires His Word to be the center of *everyone's* life. Jesus emphasized this in His Word when He said, *"If you abide in My word, you are My disciples indeed. And you shall know the truth, and the truth shall make you free"* (John 8:31–32).

What does it mean to *"abide"* in the Word of God? It is meditation—memorizing, personalizing, and visualizing the Word of God. You never have to worry about whether the sun will rise in the morning or whether the moon will shine at night. Do you realize God's Word placed the sun and the moon where they are? It also keeps them there. Hebrews 1:3 says that God is *"upholding all things by the word of His power."* Continuing in the Word is very important; meditating on the Word of God is extremely important. If it is powerful enough to uphold the sun and the moon, as it did for Joshua, then it is powerful enough to take care of you.

When I first read the book of Ezra, my immediate thought was: *This is a marvelous book. Why has it taken me so long to get into something this commanding and mighty?* It demonstrates the power of the Word in the lives of individuals and nations, and it has the ability to change the entire world.

The story opens in a part of Israel's history that is critical. Before we can thoroughly understand it, however, we need to look at the events that preceded it. Joshua and his men took the Promised Land in only six-and-a-half years. Joshua was a man who meditated on the Word and didn't let it depart from his mouth. He was obedient.

The book of Judges follows Joshua and describes the early government of Israel. Then, the Bible gives the history of kings—both good and bad—and the prophets' ministry to the kings.

As we read, we see that Israel consisted of two separate kingdoms: the northern and the southern kingdoms. During this period, the Israelites began to lean increasingly on the repulsive idols of the heathen people in the land. God repeatedly warned the people of Israel about this danger, before He finally decided that enough was enough. He led King Nebuchadnezzar and the Assyrian nation in battle against the northern kingdom of Israel, and they were taken captive.

Several years later, the southern kingdom was attacked by the Babylonians, and they, too, were taken into captivity. All of Israel had been taken captive, even though, years before, the prophet

Jeremiah had warned them what would happen if they did not repent.

God had used Jeremiah to tell the Jews about the horrendous penalties of idolatry. He used a group of people called the Rechabites as a visual aid in His message of warning. The Rechabites were descendants of a man named Jonadab, who had lived two hundred years prior. God gave Jonadab specific orders:

1. Don't bow down to idols

2. Don't plant vineyards

3. Be nomadic and do not buy land

4. Don't drink of the vine

Jonadab taught these rule to his children, his children's children, and so on. The Rechabites never owned land. For two hundred years, they wandered the northern kingdom with their sheep and goats and never drank wine or planted vineyards.

When Assyria attacked Israel's northern kingdom, the Rechabites weren't there. Since the area had dried up, they had taken their flocks and wandered into the southern kingdom. By doing so, they avoided the Assyrian captivity. The prophet Jeremiah warned the southern kingdom that they would taken captive by the Babylonians if they did not obey God's commands.

Jeremiah set pots on a table and filled them with wine. Then he invited all of the Rechabite leaders living in Judah to join him. "Have a drink," he told them. The Rechabites replied, "Jeremiah, you know we don't drink. God spoke to Jonadab two hundred years ago and told us not to drink. Since that day, we have never tasted of the vine." (See Jeremiah 35:5–6.)

God was using Jeremiah's demonstration to mercifully warn the people of Judah. He was saying, in effect, "Do you see that the Rechabites have obeyed My Word for two hundred years? They have never tasted of the vine, never planted vineyards, and never bought land. Now, because they have obeyed the Word, it is going to profit them."

Did you know that the Word of God is always profitable? This is right in line with the message of Joshua 1:8—the Word brings good success.

The Rechabites weren't taken captive when King Nebuchadnezzar led the Babylonians into the southern kingdom. When Nebuchadnezzar invaded, he said, "Anybody who owns land goes into captivity. Anybody who doesn't own land can stay here." And the Rechabites stayed. What can we learn from the prophet Jeremiah's message? "It pays to do what the Word says."

The Israelites were captured, and so were the people of Judah. Many of them were slaves, but don't get the idea that all of them were groveling in the ground. There were those who held esteemed positions. Ezra held a high court position, as did Nehemiah. During this same time, Esther was a queen. Notice that these Israelites were devoted servants of the Lord. When you are obedient to God, He can take care of you no matter where you are. Later, when the time came to return to Israel, many of the Jews in Babylon were so wealthy, they chose not to return. We see this in the New Testament, when the apostle Peter preached to the church at Babylon, to the Jews who had never returned to Israel.

Meditation in Captivity

Before the Israelites were taken into captivity, Jeremiah prophesied that they would be captive for seventy years.

"And this whole land shall be a desolation and an astonishment, and these nations shall serve the king of Babylon seventy years. Then it will come to pass, when seventy years are

completed, that I will punish the king of Babylon and that nation, the land of the Chaldeans, for their iniquity," says the LORD; *"and I will make it a perpetual desolation."*

(Jeremiah 25:11–12)

What were the Jews in Babylon thinking during all that time? For the most part, they had their minds fastened on the Word of God. They remembered the words of the prophet: In seventy years, we get to go back. Jeremiah's prophecy was a hope, a strength, and a comfort to all those who were in captivity. We, too, have a hope, a strength, and a comfort; we can fasten our hearts on what the glorious Word has said about Jesus' return. That is a sustaining hope; and we are to comfort one another with the hope of Jesus' return. We don't know the day or the hour, but Jesus is coming back. The New Testament says that this hope is purifying. (See 1 John 3:3.)

When your thoughts are fastened to the Word of God, you are involved in a form of meditation, and the truth will both keep and sustain you.

In captivity, the children of Israel kept and obeyed God's Word to remain pure in their intent toward God. I'm sure that when the seventieth year arrived, many said, "What's going to happen? God said seventy years, and His Word cannot fail."

God had already started to prepare for the seventieth year, when His people would return to their Promised Land. I became excited when I saw how He had begun to prepare for this event one hundred fifty years earlier, through the prophet Isaiah:

Who says of Cyrus, "He is My shepherd, and he shall perform all My pleasure, saying to Jerusalem, 'You shall be built,' and to the temple, 'Your foundation shall be laid.'" Thus says the LORD *to His anointed, to Cyrus, whose right hand I have held; to subdue nations before him and loose the armor of kings, to open before him the double doors, so that the gates*

will not be shut: "I will go before you and make the crooked
places straight; I will break in pieces the gates of bronze and
cut the bars of iron. I will give you the treasures of darkness
and hidden riches of secret places, that you may know that I,
the Lord, *who call you by your name, am the God of Israel."*

(Isaiah 44:28–45:3)

In this prophecy, Isaiah prophesied about a man named Cyrus, a man chosen by God to set the Israelites free after their seventy-year captivity in Babylon. Before the kingdom of Babylon had ever been built, Isaiah prophesied in this passage that Cyrus would subdue that nation, which he did! Then Isaiah even described what Babylon would look like in a vision. Herodotus, supposedly the most credible historian of the Babylonian captivity, wrote that the city had two-leaved gates with bars of iron, as mentioned in the prophecy.

Why would God name Cyrus, long before his birth, and tell him that he would subdue the Babylonian kingdom? Why tell him that He would allow the temple to be rebuilt in Jerusalem? The answer is in this Scripture:

...that you may know that I, the Lord, *who call you by your*
name, am the God of Israel. For Jacob My servant's sake,
and Israel My elect, I have even called you by your name; I
have named you, though you have not known Me.

(Isaiah 45:3–4)

God was saying, in effect, "Cyrus, I called you by name one hundred fifty years ago so that you would know that I ordained you to be the man who frees My people. You are going to free them after seventy years, according to what Jeremiah prophesied. Then you will let them rebuild Jerusalem and the temple."

Cyrus was a Persian, not a Jew. Why would he want the Jewish temple to be rebuilt? Josephus, a Jewish historian, claimed that somebody brought the book of Isaiah to Cyrus and said, "Your name is in this book."

Cyrus must have said, "Is it really? Let me see." Then, the person showed Cyrus the Scriptures and said, "The seventy years are over; you're supposed to let us return to Jerusalem and build the temple." According to Josephus, Cyrus was impressed, and he allowed the Israelites to be freed.

Josephus stated,

For he stirred up the mind of Cyrus, and made him write this throughout all Asia: "Thus saith Cyrus the king: Since God Almighty hath appointed me to be king of the habitable earth, I believe that he is that God which the nation of the Israelites worship; for indeed he foretold my name by the prophets, and that I should build him a house at Jerusalem, in the country of Judea."[2]

The Bible concurs.

Now in the first year of Cyrus king of Persia, that the word of the LORD by the mouth of Jeremiah might be fulfilled, the LORD stirred up the spirit of Cyrus king of Persia, so that he made a proclamation throughout all his kingdom, and also put it in writing, saying, thus says Cyrus king of Persia: All the kingdoms of the earth the LORD God of heaven has given me. And He has commanded me to build Him a house at Jerusalem which is in Judah. (Ezra 1:1–2)

What stirred Cyrus' heart? What motivated him to release the captive Israelites to return to Jerusalem? The Word of God moved Cyrus.

---

2. Flavius Josephus, *The Works of Josephus, Complete and Unabridged* (Nashville, TN: Thomas Nelson Publishers, 1998), 286.

> *Who is among you of all His people? May his God be with*
> *him, and let him go up to Jerusalem which is in Judah, and*
> *build the house of the LORD God of Israel.*   (Ezra 1:3)

Cyrus not only said, "Go back to Jerusalem and rebuild the temple"; he also said, "Any remaining Jews will pay money to help those who are going."

> *King Cyrus also brought out the articles of the house of the*
> *LORD, which Nebuchadnezzar had taken from Jerusalem*
> *and put in the temple of his gods; and Cyrus king of Persia*
> *brought them out by the hand of Mithredath the treasurer,*
> *and counted them out to Sheshbazzar the prince of Judah.*
>   (verses 7–8)

King Cyrus gave the Jews all sorts of wealth to take back to Judah with them. I think God must have been saying, in effect, "Ha, ha, ha. Persia is going to pay the expenses of rebuilding the temple in Jerusalem." It was just like the Egyptians paying for the tabernacle when the Israelites brought their gold from Egypt during their exodus.

Then, Ezra chapter 2 describes how all of the people prepared to go back to Judah. They divided the people by tribes, by priesthoods, and by cities, and if someone didn't know quite where they belonged, they went in a special lot, too. When they were ready to go, there were about 300,000 of them.

This was a tremendous trip. For one thing, they had to travel way up north in order to follow the Euphrates River down through Syria and into Jerusalem. It was a journey of around one thousand miles; it took them four months to complete. Nebuchadnezzar had taken captive 600,000 Jews, and this did not include the people taken captive by the Assyrians in the northern kingdom. Certainly, people died during those seventy years; but babies were born. Still, many Jews chose not to leave Babylon, unwilling to start from scratch all over again.

When the Jews arrived in Judah, they encountered many enemies, people who had settled into the area. They were the Ammonites, Edomites, Moabites, Egyptians, and mongrel Jews, who had intermarried with some of the Assyrians (this is how the Samaritan race began to emerge).

When the Jews arrived and found people living in their land, they were unhappy and felt threatened.

> *Though fear had come upon them because of the people of those countries, they set the altar on its bases; and they offered burnt offerings on it to the LORD, both the morning and evening burnt offerings.* (Ezra 3:3)

Notice the Jews' spiritual behavior after spending seventy years with their thoughts on the Word of God. The first thing they said was, "We need to build an altar, and God will protect us." I love that. When I read it, I thought, *They are seeking first the kingdom of God.*

These people fastened their minds to the word that came through the prophets Isaiah and Jeremiah. As they travelled that arduous long distance, what had they been doing? Obeying and fulfilling the Word of God, which had stirred their hearts.

God stirred the heart of Cyrus, and He stirred the hearts of the Israelites—with His Word. Whenever the Word supports anything, you know the foundation is secure. The Israelites built an altar, demonstrating their trust in the Lord. They started building the foundation for the temple. After it was built, there were mixed reactions. The old men cried, "Oh, this isn't the way that it used to be. It won't be as gorgeous as Solomon's temple was." (See Ezra 3:12.) They remembered how things had been in the past. However, the young men shouted for joy. "We're fulfilling the Word of God," they cried out. (See Ezra 3:13.)

When I read this, I was reminded of something I've seen in church. I've heard older people say similar things: "These days just aren't like the days when we tarried all night for the baptism of the Holy Spirit." "These people must not have what we received." That really bugs me, because the Bible says we don't receive anything through works, but only through faith. It is acting on the Word that brings anything from God. The older men were really saying, "This just isn't like the good old days." And the young men probably said, "Shut up. That's not faith; stop looking back."

It must have been an exciting adventure to be involved in the rebuilding of the temple. But then the enemy stepped in. After the temple's foundation was laid, the idolatrous people said, "*Let us build with you, for we seek your God as you do*" (Ezra 4:2). These were the mongrel Jews, along with the Ammonites, the Edomites, the Moabites, and the Egyptians, none of whom were supposed to take any part in the work of God. These people were not just saying that they wanted to help; they also wanted to bring in all of their idols, and that scared the Jews. No Jew wanted these idolaters to help. They thought, *We were sent to Babylon for seventy years because of idolatry. We don't want to go back.*

The Babylonian captivity did one thing in particular for the Jewish people. It cured them of idolatry forever, for they never involved themselves in it again. They told the people, "*You may do nothing with us to build a house for our God; but we alone will build to the Lord God of Israel, as King Cyrus the king of Persia has commanded us*" (Ezra 4:3).

The others were enraged, and the Bible says that they sat and wrote to the Persian king. The Persians tended to change kings like they changed clothes—there were three different rulers in the book of Ezra alone, and the time span wasn't long.

In the days of Artaxerxes also, Bishlam, Mithredath, Tabel, and the rest of their companions wrote to Artaxerxes king of Persia; and the letter was written in Aramaic script, and translated into the Aramaic language. (Ezra 4:7)

They were saying, "Dear King Artaxerxes, do you know what the Jews are doing down here? They are rebuilding their temple. The next thing you know, they'll rebuild the walls. After that, it'll be a fortress; and before you know it, they'll rebel against you. Have you looked at the Jews' history? They're a rebellious people!"

The letter never mentioned King Cyrus' decree for the temple's rebuilding, and Artaxerxes didn't look for it. Instead, he wrote back, saying,

Now give the command to make these men cease, that this city may not be built until the command is given by me. Take heed now that you do not fail to do this. Why should damage increase to the hurt of the kings? Now when the copy of King Artaxerxes' letter was read before Rehum, Shimshai the scribe, and their companions, they went up in haste to Jerusalem against the Jews, and by force of arms made them cease. (Ezra 4:21–23)

In other words, Artaxerxes said, "Stop those Jews right now. Don't let them build one more thing. Nothing."

When the Israelites received the letter, they were discouraged and said, "Well, what's the use?" And they stopped building the temple. They were not standing on the Word at the time, and when that happens, people tend to look only at the circumstances, and they get in to trouble. They could have responded by saying, "Dear Artaxerxes, look up Cyrus's decree. We have permission to rebuild the temple." Instead, they fell apart.

That is bad news. Here's the good news: Although you may delay God's plan, you'll never do away with it. God's Word *will be* fulfilled.

For fifteen years, the Israelites stayed in Judah and had a pity party. Pity, by the way, is faith's worst enemy. They said, in effect, "We came all this distance with our children, and we can't build the temple."

Was God's Word going to get the temple built? As I read this, I thought, *If God called Cyrus by his name one hundred fifty years before he was born, His Word would complete the rebuilding of the temple. These people didn't stop God's plan; they only delayed it. And that wouldn't have happened if they had been meditating on His Word.*

During that time, God raised up two men to complete the task of rebuilding of the temple. Their names were Haggai and Zechariah. The books of Haggai and Zechariah become easier to understand when you realize they were prophesying to the people about finishing the mission. Reading the prophetic books can confuse people because they don't know the timeline of events. That is why it is easier to understand the Bible by reading it chronologically rather than in the order they've been placed in the Old Testament.

The prophet Haggai was an older man who had seen Solomon's temple. He said, "You know God's Word told you to complete this temple." Haggai prophesied positive words and greatly stirred the peoples' hearts. Because Haggai was a contemporary of the older people, they could not say, "Well, these kids just want to do their own thing." They had to receive his prophecies. But look at God's provision: Had He raised up only an older prophet, the young people would have written him off as an old man, dreaming dreams. But they couldn't say that because God raised up another prophet, a younger man named Zechariah, who not only had prophecies, but who also had visions.

When Haggai and Zechariah prophesied together, the Word of God touched those people and stirred their hearts. They thought, *Why aren't we building the temple, as God commanded?*

What happens when the Word of God stirs you? It triggers faith, and faith brings action. When you have faith in the Word, there will be movement, because faith produces works.

By the time the prophesying through Haggai and Zechariah took place, Persia had another king, and the Israelites wrote him a letter saying, "We have permission to rebuild the temple." They explained,

> *In the first year of Cyrus king of Babylon, King Cyrus issued a decree to build this house of God. Also, the gold and silver articles of the house of God, which Nebuchadnezzar had taken from the temple that was in Jerusalem and carried into the temple of Babylon; those King Cyrus took from the temple of Babylon, and they were given to one named Sheshbazzar, whom he had made governor.* (Ezra 5:13–14)

The letter said, "Dear King Darius, we're here in Israel, and King Cyrus told us to build this temple. He even gave us money for it. We laid the foundation. Even the mongrel Jews, Egyptians, Ammonites, Moabites, and Edomites wanted to help build and bring in their idols, but we're not supposed to let them help. So, they told us to stop building and wrote a letter to King Artaxerxes, making us look bad. He told us not to build, but we already had a decree from King Cyrus. Look it up, because we're going to obey King Cyrus."

Darius looked up the decree.

> *Then King Darius issued a decree, and a search was made in the archives, where the treasures were stored in Babylon. And at Achmetha, in the palace that is in the province of Media,*

a scroll was found, and in it a record was written thus: in the
first year of King Cyrus, King Cyrus issued a decree concern-
ing the house of God at Jerusalem: "Let the house be rebuilt,
the place where they offered sacrifices; and let the foundations
of it be firmly laid."   (Ezra 6:1–3)

What happened when Darius finally found these instructions
from King Cyrus? His heart was stirred. He wrote back and said,

Let the work of this house of God alone; let the governor of the
Jews and the elders of the Jews build this house of God on its site.
Moreover I issue a decree as to what you shall do for the elders
of these Jews, for the building of this house of God: let the cost be
paid at the king's expense from taxes on the region beyond the
river; this is to be given immediately to these men, so that they
are not hindered. And whatever they need; young bulls, rams,
and lambs for the burnt offerings of the God of heaven, wheat,
salt, wine, and oil, according to the request of the priests who are
in Jerusalem; let it be given them day by day without fail, that
they may offer sacrifices of sweet aroma to the God of heaven,
and pray for the life of the king and his sons.   (Ezra 6:7–10)

He was asking all the non-Jews to start giving the Jews food
and animals for their burnt offerings, that they might offer sacrifices unto God. Then, he even asked the Israelites to pray for him
and his children.

Also I issue a decree that whoever alters this edict, let a timber
be pulled from his house and erected, and let him be hanged
on it; and let his house be made a refuse heap because of this.
                                                          (Ezra 6:11)

Darius directed his attention to the enemies of the Jews,
saying, "The rest of you down there, you'd better stop giving them
trouble. We'll hang you if you don't stop."

When you put faith in God and His Word, circumstances will change. Haggai and Zechariah caused the Israelites to have active faith in the Word, so their circumstances had to line up accordingly. God will even move people around, if necessary. In fact, I am often shocked at how God moves people around. For instance, look at how He dealt with the heart of a young man named Ezra:

> *For Ezra had prepared his heart to seek the Law of the LORD, and to do it, and to teach statutes and ordinances in Israel. This is a copy of the letter that King Artaxerxes gave Ezra the priest, the scribe, expert in the words of the commandments of the LORD, and of His statutes to Israel.* (Ezra 7:10–11)

Ezra was a priest, living in Babylon, who had never been in the temple; he had never made a sacrifice, and yet his first love was the law of the Lord. He must have thought, *If the Word isn't there, the people will return to idolatry.* Ezra prepared his heart to seek God through meditation, teaching, and obeying the Word of God. Then the Lord gave Ezra a burden for the hearts of the people who would worship there. He knew that the people had to be given the Word of God, or they would not endure against their enemies.

I examined historical accounts, because it often helps to make biblical stories more clear. I don't consider history to be divine; it isn't the Word of God, but it can provide helpful insights into the Bible. Historians say that when Nebuchadnezzar seized Judah, he took copies of the law, the Psalms, the Proverbs, and other poetical books, and burned them. He didn't want God's Word to enter Babylon.

But you can't destroy the Word of God, can you? One hundred years ago, someone said, "In twenty years, there won't be a Bible." You can't listen to such ridiculous talk. God knows how to protect His Word. There will always be people predicting kooky things like that, but the Bible is a worldwide best seller.

Though Nebuchadnezzar attempted to destroy God's Word, someone smuggled a copy of the Hebrew Scriptures into Babylon—it must have been a large portion of the Old Testament. It would not have contained the books of Ezra, Nehemiah, Haggai, Zechariah, or Malachi, of course, but it probably contained three-fourths of our current Old Testament. Historic accounts tell us what the wonderful priest Ezra did. He *memorized* all of it.

Ezra had a tremendous devotion to the Word of God. His name means "help." (Anybody who is as full of the Word of God as Ezra was will always be a help in any situation.) Ezra was the first scribe of the Bible. Scribes were the people who copied down God's Word. It is said that Ezra memorized the Scriptures, wrote them all down, and divided it into the Pentateuch, the historical and poetical books, the prophetical books, and so on. Ezra was the first one to categorize the Word of God; he was stirred and motivated by the Word, and he wanted the rest of the Israelites to be stirred and motivated by it, too.

He talked to the king and requested permission to return to Judah to bring God's Word to the Israelites. The king granted his consent; but that's not all he gave Ezra—he also gave him great wealth and gold to refurbish the temple. Ezra accepted these bountiful gifts, and he told the king, "There is no use in my returning to Jerusalem alone. The Word of God is in my heart, but I want to pour it into the hearts of the priests, so that they will pour it into the people's hearts."

Ezra made a call for the Jews to go back to Judah with him, and around five thousand made the journey. But among them were no priests. This disturbed Ezra. He wanted successors who would take hold of the Word. He told the people to rouse the priests, and, finally, about forty-five priests answered the call. Then Ezra said, "We will also need protection," and he called the people to fast and pray.

Isaiah 58, one of the most well-known fasting chapters in the Bible, says that fasting brings a reward, *"The glory of the* LORD *shall be your rear guard"* (Isaiah 58:8). Notice that it says that the glory of the Lord will be your *rear* guard; it protects the back of you. Ephesians chapter 6 tells Christians how to put on the armor of the Lord, a protection for the front of the body. But fasting brings protection from sneak attacks by covering the back. I believe strongly in regular weekly fasting; and I think Christians can take a lesson from Ezra's steadfast faithfulness.

Prayer Meditation

Meanwhile, Haggai and Zechariah were prophesying, and the people began to turn to the Word of God. While they were building the temple, they sang Psalm 136:1–3 as they worked:

Oh, give thanks to the LORD, *for He is good! For His mercy endures forever. Oh, give thanks to the God of gods! For His mercy endures forever. Oh, give thanks to the Lord of lords! For His mercy endures forever.*

The rest of Psalm 136 rehearses what God had done for the Israelites. They were singing that song as a way of saying, "God, You helped us then, and You are helping us now." All the time they were building, the song went on, reminding them that God performed His Word in the past, and He was performing it in the present.

Again, here is prayer that says:

To Him who laid out the earth above the waters, for His mercy endures forever; to Him who made great lights, for His mercy endures forever; the sun to rule by day, for His mercy endures forever; the moon and stars to rule by night,

*for His mercy endures forever. To Him who struck Egypt in
their firstborn, for His mercy endures forever; and brought out
Israel from among them, for His mercy endures forever; with
a strong hand, and with an outstretched arm, for His mercy
endures forever; to Him who divided the Red Sea in two, for
His mercy endures forever.*   (Psalm 136:6–13)

That is an effective prayer. It's scriptural to pray the way the
Israelites did. This type of prayer is another form of meditation.

Meditating on What You Hear

When Ezra arrived in Judah with the Jews who traveled with
him, he delivered treasures to the house of God. Then he gath-
ered the people and started reading the Word to them. He made
everybody stand while he read, and he continued for three hours.
Do you think your preacher is longwinded? You wouldn't if you
listened to Ezra. The listeners had not heard the Word of God for
a many years. All the men, women, and children stood for hours,
listening intently, as Ezra poured it into their hearts.

I have always been interested in the way priests and kings were
instructed to handle the Word of God; God wants His people to
have the same reverence for His Word.

First, priests were responsible to write down all of the
Scriptures, as Ezra had done. Then, they were to carry the Word
behind their breastplate, and when someone had a problem, they
would pull out the Word and tell them what it said.

When kings were placed in office, they went to the priest and
said, "Give me your copy of the Bible." (See Deuteronomy 17, 23,
31.) Then they would personally transcribe the Bible, making their
own copy. The king was to read it every day, so he could judge the
people appropriately. God always wanted to be the center of men's

lives. He wanted His Word in a prevalent position, so the people would not get in to trouble.

Every seven years, the priest was supposed to stand before the people, as Ezra had done, and read all of the words that had been written. What was the seventh year? It was very special:

> So Moses wrote this law and delivered it to the priests, the sons of Levi, who bore the ark of the covenant of the LORD, and to all the elders of Israel. And Moses commanded them, saying: "At the end of every seven years, at the appointed time in the year of release, at the Feast of Tabernacles, when all Israel comes to appear before the LORD your God in the place which He chooses, you shall read this law before all Israel in their hearing."
> (Deuteronomy 31:9–11)

Notice they read these Scriptures during the year of release. What did Jesus say? "If you abide in My word, you are My disciples indeed. And you shall know the truth, and the truth shall make you free" (John 8:31–32). That is exactly what Ezra was doing; he was releasing the people from bondage by reading them God's Word.

As he read, the mongrel Jews were convicted. They said, "We've been doing some wrong things. We haven't been living right; we've lived with these idolatrous women, and we want to separate ourselves from them."

The Word of God does so many things, doesn't it? What was happening here? It was the washing of the water of the Word. The Word began cleansing the people from sin, and a real revival started.

The Word of God brought the captives home and rebuilt their temple; the Word of God was their protection, their refreshing and cleansing. What happened? It released them.

Every time I see Ezra's name, I think, "God bless you, Ezra." He loved the Word of God so much that he memorized it so it couldn't be destroyed. Then, he wrote it down and gave it to the people. It was passed on from generation to generation and was given to you and me.

Where to Meditate for You and Me

I find that you can meditate in any place you set your heart to do so.

One time, I was on a very early flight to Casper, Wyoming. I was meditating on Proverbs 11:30, "*The fruit of the righteous is a tree of life, and he who wins souls is wise.*" As I was spiritually chewing on these words, the Lord spoke to my spirit. saying, *Wouldn't you like to win a soul to Christ?*

I looked around the plane. At that early hour, almost every seat was vacant. I thought, *Who, Lord?*

His response to me was, *How about the flight attendant?*

As she served coffee, God opened her heart to the *Four Spiritual Laws* tract,[3] which I had studied earlier.

You may find that the same Scriptures you meditate on one day will be used in fantastic ways that same day. I've discovered that if you really desire something, you will whatever is required to attain it. If you want to be successful in every area of life, then you'd better meditate on the Word of God. Perhaps you can't start out memorizing five verses a day; but you can learn one verse every other day, can't you?

When God told Joshua to meditate on the Word, He was saying, "I want you to be saturated, completely soaked, with the

---

3. Bill Bright, *The Four Spiritual Laws* (Peachtree City, GA: Campus Crusade for Christ, 2007).

Word of God: keep it in your mind, your mouth, and your actions." Joshua became an example of God's living Word in action—and so can you. Joshua was over eighty, and a very busy man, as we've seen. As I studied him, I thought, *I wonder what he meditated on. Did he pick Proverbs?*

The first year I began meditating God's Word, I memorized Proverbs. It was so exciting that I thought everybody should memorize them. I even made my children start memorizing the book. My son really complained, saying, "There isn't a mother in our church that's making her kids memorize the book of Proverbs." Then, he really started crying the blues. He said, "There isn't a mother in this city that makes her children memorize Proverbs. I doubt there's a mother in the nation!" I decided to stop him before he got to the world, so I said, "Oh, honey, how fortunate you are to have me for your mother. You have the only mother in the nation who makes you memorize. Aren't you pleased?"

The only books that were written when Joshua meditated on Scripture were the first five books of the Bible, or the Pentateuch (or Torah), which was written by Moses and consisted of Genesis, Exodus, Leviticus, Numbers, and Deuteronomy. How would you like to memorize Leviticus? Yet that is what Joshua meditated on, day and night.

Once when I was teaching on meditation, a man came up to me after the service and said, "Marilyn, I am eighty-three years old. I started meditating on God's Word when I was twenty-six." He started quoting chapter after chapter of the gospel of Matthew. I listened to him quoting the Word, and I cannot tell you what happened to me spiritually. It seemed as though my spirit jumped up and said, "Whee!" The Bible says that hearing the Word brings faith. My hearing of the meditated Word of God coming out of that man's mouth was "faith hearing."

I asked him, "Are you retired?"

"Retired? Do I look retired? I am a professor at a university, and I'll never retire. I'll teach until I die."

I thought, *Of course. All of the Word inside of him is filling him, jam-packed with God's life.* That man was also prosperous in every single area. I thought, *Oh God, I wish I'd started meditating at the age of twenty-six.* It's like exercise; it's never too late to begin.

The bathtub is a good place to say your Scriptures aloud. Sometimes, I ride a bike and rehearse them. David meditated on his bed. (See Psalm 63:6.) Everyone has a perfect place.

5

THE "HOW" OF MEDITATION:

I want to share what I wrote about my method of meditation in my recent book *Your Pathway to Miracles*:

> The following is the method I used. I took Proverbs 6:22 as my guide, which talks about taking the teachings of one's parents to heart: "*When you walk, they will guide you; when you sleep, they will watch over you; when you awake, they will speak to you*" (NIV).
>
> I decided to begin in the morning, corresponding to the phrase, "*When you awake, they will speak to you.*" So, when I got up each day, I would say my memory verse ten times.
>
> In the afternoon, I would say the verse one time, in conjunction with the phrase, "*When you walk, they will guide you.*"
>
> Then, at night, I would recite my verse once before going to bed, and I would say the verse for the next day one time,

in relation to the phrase, *"When you sleep, they will watch over you."* It's been said that the last thing you hear at night goes through your mind seven times.[4]

The Absolute First

As I said earlier, as you get out of bed, your mind is at its freshest and cleanest. It's like a blackboard without writing. Why waste it on anything other than God's Word? Even before I brush my teeth, I meditate on the Word. Because your mind is uncluttered with cares and thoughts, you'll find that you begin to grasp the Scriptures as never before.

Then, sometime during the day, review the Scriptures again and ponder them. Say them aloud, several times. Refresh your mind as to what you're memorizing.

Later, before you go to sleep, say them in bed. Say them several times. Let's review that passage from Proverbs that we read in chapter 2. These are precious verses that explain how the Scriptures will rule your spirit when you meditate on them:

> *My son, keep your father's command, and do not forsake the law of your mother. Bind them continually upon your heart; tie them around your neck. When you roam, they will lead you; when you sleep, they will keep you; and when you awake, they will speak with you.*
> (Proverbs 6:20–22)

The Word of God will keep you. I believe that when God's Word is continually fresh in your spirit through meditation, it will protect you throughout the day and during the night.

---

4. Marilyn Hickey, *Your Pathway to Miracles* (New Kensington, PA: Whitaker House, 2011), 76.

Select the Material

The first step in getting started with meditation is to select the book of the Bible you want to study. Notice I said *book*, not *verse* or *chapter*. There are plenty of short books, if you don't want to tackle one of the longer ones. You might begin with Jude or Colossians.

For this book, I have included verses arranged by topic that can prepare you to memorize entire books of the Bible. I started memorizing by learning a verse each day. Even that small amount of Scripture quickened my mind, and I began increasing the amount I memorized. Eventually, I was up to fifteen verses each day. The Word of God will quicken you, so don't get discouraged. Start small, and you can be assured that your meditation will grow easier, if you stick with it. Think of it as a physical exercise. You begin with a few push-ups or a short jog, and then you gradually increase your workout each day until, before you know it, you are buff and running long distances.

After you've selected the material, choose the number of verses you want to learn for that day. Start with an amount that is comfortable for you, even if it's only a verse each day. Be sure to set a daily goal for yourself and consistently meet those goals.

Choose a Partner

I think having a partner is wonderful. Lately, my busy travel schedule has made it hard for me to meditate with same partner, but I've had some great partners over the years. I would recommend that you choose one. You don't need to have long conversations each day, just go over your verses together. When you know that you have to call your partner in the morning with memorized Scripture, you'll be more diligent about it. Even when your mind is tired and fuzzy, you'll get those Scriptures in.

I won't kid you. There are times when you'll feel discouraged. Some days, the devil says to me, *Why are you going through all this effort? What are you trying to accomplish?* But if you have a partner, you will have someone to encourage you when your meditation becomes a struggle.

When I meditated on the book of Proverbs, I breezed through a few chapters. Then I got to a chapter that was a struggle to get through. I found the same thing happened when I read some of the psalms. Psalms 63 and 64 were easy, but another chapter made me wonder whether I'd ever get through it. A partner will help you keep the pace when you're discouraged. If you fall behind, that's okay. Fall behind. You have the rest of your life.

A Chapter at a Time

I like to meditate on one chapter at a time before I go on to the next. I do not totally review a book. I'm not memorizing so that I can say, "I can quote thirty-one chapters of Proverbs, if you have enough time." The purpose of meditation is to get the Word into your spirit so that it can become wisdom in your life. If I'm learning four verses at a time, and the chapter has twelve verses, then I'll have memorized the whole chapter on the third day.

Refresh Past Meditations

Wherever I happen to be meditating, I like to read a verse from books that I've meditated on previously. When you finish one book and move on to another, look back occasionally and review what you've meditated on in the past.

Why meditate on the Word? Because God said it would bring success into every area of your life. God's Word is going to dominate your thought life, your emotional responses, and your attitudes. You will be, as Joshua was, a living epistle to others. When someone talks with you, the Holy Spirit will begin quickening those memorized Scriptures to your mind, and you'll think, *He needs this Scripture; it just fits him.*

Keep a Notebook

This is another practice you'll find both helpful and encouraging. Carry around a small notebook and write down the revelations the Lord gives to you. If you don't write them down, you'll likely forget them. Through meditation, you'll discover that your spirit becomes more alive than ever before, and a notebook will come in handy to record those moments of fresh revelation. Because you are making the Word of God precious in your life, you'll find the Lord revealing more to you than ever before. If you're ever in a place of discouragement regarding your memorization, read your notebook past revelations, and let them be an encouragement.

Prescription of Meditation

My soul shall be satisfied as with marrow and fatness, and my mouth shall praise You with joyful lips. When I remember You on my bed, I meditate on You in the night watches.
(Psalm 63:5–6)

People will say to me, "I'm starving for the Word in my church. I get no spiritual food, and my pastor isn't much of a preacher." Psalm 63 says you are supposed to remember the Lord and meditate on *Him*; don't rely on your pastor for all of your spiritual food. This Scripture says your soul will get *fat* and your mouth will be *full of praise* when you meditate on the Lord.

Notice, too, that the psalmist's meditation was at night. Have you ever noticed that problems seem to loom ten times larger at night? I'm not one to wake up in the middle of the night, but when I do, it's usually because of a difficult circumstance. It's then that my problems look like mountains. That's the time to meditate on the Word of God.

At a seminar in Schenectady, New York, I remember thinking that every possible thing that could go wrong seemed to be hitting me all at once: finances, family, radio ministry, and so on. I also had a terrible pain and a swollen area, from which red streaks were starting to appear. I prayed, and said, "I am not going to be moved by those symptoms." I went through my memory verses, but I still could not sleep because of the pain.

When I travel, I carry audio versions of the New Testament with me, and I finally said, "All right, devil, you're going to be sorry for keeping me awake." After about an hour of listening to the Word, the soothing quality of it caused me to fall back asleep. I turned the cassette off and said, "Father, it's not my problem. I cast my cares on You."

In the morning, there weren't any red streaks, and two days later, the swelling was gone, too. The Word works.

As I noted in the beginning, Psalm 119:11 says, *"Your word I have hidden in my heart, that I might not sin against You!"* Fair enough. The action, *hiding the word*, and the reason, *so as not to sin against God*, are captured in this one short verse. How do we do this?

Again, here are a few simple tips:

1. Gather a collection of Scripture passages you desire to meditate upon. I would suggest the books Ephesians or Colossians. (I began with Proverbs and loved every minute spent there.) Or, as I stated, you can start with a few verses. I have included some examples for you later in the book.

2. Decide on a certain portion to memorize each day—
   one verse a day, one verse every other day, or two
   verses. Begin at a comfortable pace.

3. Select a partner, someone who desires to meditate
   on the same material. Call your partner daily and
   rehearse the Scripture. Keep your telephone conversation short.

I want to stop here and take a moment to share an experience
about one of my previous prayer partners. When I started to meditate, I decided I needed to find a partner. I thought that in case I
ever felt the urge to stop meditating, or I became discouraged, a
partner would keep me encouraged. It seemed like a good way to
start; so I prayed, "Lord, who would You have me to be partners
with?" The Lord spoke to me, and it was not the person I wanted
Him to choose. It was a person who attended our church, who
tended to gripe a lot. Whenever she came in the room, you felt like
you wanted to be somewhere else, because if she got hold of you, it
took half an hour for her to tell you all of her problems. Then she'd
look you up later, because she hadn't finished telling you about
them.

The Lord said to me, *I want her to be your meditation partner.*

I thought, *Oh Lord, anybody but her.* I thought she would
spend the time griping, and we wouldn't be able to get through the
verses. Then I thought, *Oh, she'll probably say no.* So, I called and
said, "For the rest of my life, I'm going to meditate on the Word of
God. I'll start in Proverbs, and I would like you to be my partner
for that book, if you will."

"Yes," she said. "I want to be your partner."

I arranged to call her at seven each morning and told her I
wouldn't be able to talk for very long because my children had to
go to school.

The next morning, when I called, she immediately started griping.

"Let's go over our verses," I said.

"No," she answered. "I need to tell you this first. I am so depressed."

"I don't have time, because my children have to get to school," I replied, and we proceeded to go over our Bible verses.

Over the next two weeks, every time I called this lady, she wanted to gripe, but I didn't have time for griping, so we would go over Scriptures we wanted to meditate on, and that's all. By the third week, however, something had happened. I called her the first morning of the third week, and instead of griping, this lady said, "I got the most marvelous thing out of this chapter. Did you get this?" Then she shared the revelation she received from the Word, and it was so exciting. From that day forward, her whole attitude had changed.

Some time afterward, my husband asked, "What happened to that woman? She used to be the most negative person I've ever seen."

I said, "I can tell you what happened to her. The Word of God started coming out of her mouth through meditation—and it changed her." And it can change you, too.

Okay, let's continue with tips on meditation:

1. Encourage one another—especially if you get behind.

2. Keep a notebook on the revelations you receive while meditating.

3. Be sure to memorize the chapter and verse of the book you're memorizing when studying verses alone. It's good to know the where the Scripture is found.

4. Don't get discouraged.

Meditation is the way we hide the Word of God in our hearts and receive the benefits mentioned in Psalm 119:11, Joshua 1:8, and numerous other passages in the Bible.

You can hide the Word, and when you seek it, you'll find something rich and more rewarding than a child's game. You'll find the key to a blessed, prosperous, and successful life.

I'll be honest—when I began studying Joshua 1:8, I was troubled. I thought, *Lord, You are telling me here and in Psalm 1 to meditate on Your Word day and night—but have You seen my schedule? I'm busy. I'm a mother, a pastor's wife; and then there is the radio and television ministry, along with writing and traveling. How can I possibly meditate on Your Word day and night? You must not understand my schedule.* Then the Lord began dealing with me about Joshua's schedule. He said, *Did you know that Joshua was responsible for the food, water, clothing, and spiritual and military guidance for over a million people?* Think about that. While the Israelites had been in the wilderness, God provided everything: food (manna), clothing that didn't wear out, heat and air-conditioning (the pillar of cloud and fire), military protection, and water. God met every provision of the children of Israel while they were wandering in the wilderness. After they crossed the Jordan River, this provision was made Joshua's responsibility.

Joshua had a tremendous sense of accountability and a very busy schedule. The Lord said to me, *You get nervous if ten people come over for dinner. What if you had a million people to feed every day?* That's a conservative figure. I thought, *Well, Lord, if You are telling me to meditate, I'd better find out more.*

6

REST FOR
A NEW GENERATION

Symptoms of Lack of Rest

The world in which we live doesn't seem to have much rest, but it does seem to have an overflowing amount of "wrestle." We wrestle with time, schedules, demands, responsibilities, dreams, relationships, sleep, priorities, and a whole lot more. *Our lives are plagued with an abundance of wrestle, but a famine of rest.* This has spawned a whole host of crazy outcomes in our society. Such things as "road rage," ulcers, anxiety and panic attacks, obesity, addictive patterns, depression, and much more have become the new norm in our lives, even though many of them are nothing more than the banal consequences of living with a lack of rest.

To deal with these problems, we pop pills, take advice from celebrities, and obsess about our finances and lifestyles. Some even throw themselves into church or ministry work, attempting to wrestle the stress out of their lives, while neglecting their fundamental need for rest. Even God took a break after six days of creating the world, but we'll get back to that thought.

With all of this being said, you probably have picked up this book because you'd like more rest and less wrestle in your life. Such a desire could have been given to you by God, who wants you to be healthy, functional, effective, and well rested in order to fulfill the plans and designs He has for your life.

Let's consider what the absence of rest could look like in your life. Have you ever experienced any of the following things?

1. You plan your day unrealistically.

2. You're first to arrive, last to leave.

3. You're always in a hurry.

4. You make no plan for relaxation.

5. You feel guilty about doing anything other than work.

6. You view unforeseen problem as a major setback or disaster.

7. You're always thinking about several other things when working.

8. You feel a need to be recognized and you overextend yourself because of this need.[5]

These results can be a strong indication of an absence of rest, which is exactly why this book has been written—to help you live a more fulfilled and effective life, with more rest and less wrestle. With this being said, our society isn't always conducive to our need for rest. Indeed, it seems as though a well-rested person in our culture is considered to be a freak, or possibly even lazy.

---

5. https://bible.org/illustration/traits-characteristic-stress-prone.

Recently, I was on a trip to South Sudan for the Saving Moses organization; less than two weeks later, I was to visit Cambodia. Normally, when I come home from a trip, I face a hectic schedule: trying to catch up on all the work I missed, connecting with my kids in meaningful ways, and engaging with my husband beyond the essential schedule maintenance, not to mention trying to remain friendly and functional while dealing with jet lag. On this brief visit home, I experienced something quite different from my normal experience—rest. For various reasons, I was able to spend *a lot* of time with my kids and my husband, while taking a break from work in a way that afforded me time to pause and catch my breath. On more than a few occasions during this brief time home, I had to tell myself that I wasn't being lazy or irresponsible, but that God had given me this down time and it was okay to allow myself to catch my breath and be refreshed before my next trip.

From this anomalous experience, I've learned some important things about rest. Perhaps they might be useful for you, as well. But before we jump into these lessons, let's consider a few things about what rest is and what it is not.

To begin, rest isn't just about getting eight hours of sleep each night, although that can be tremendously beneficial. *Merriam-Webster's 11th Collegiate Dictionary* defines *rest* as:

1. repose, sleep

2. freedom from activity or labor

3. a state of motionless or inactivity

4. peace of mind or spirit

Recently, during a conversation at our dinner table, one of my sons suggested that everyone needs at least eight hours of sleep every night to be well rested. This statement began an interesting dialogue amongst us about the importance of sleep, of which I'm a strong advocate. But lest we be misled, let's be mindful that sleep isn't the same as rest. Indeed, I've had seasons in my life where I've had plenty of sleep, but I was anything but well rested. On the flip side, there have been a few occasions where I've been short on sleep, but still felt rested. Sleep does not necessarily equal rest, although it can be a component of rest. Additionally, I would also say that rest isn't the absence of pressures, demands, struggles, or difficulties. I've met plenty of people who manage their lives in order to remain free from stress, but they aren't rested. In fact, some of them seem quite restless compared to other people I know, who deal with pressures and demands but have learned how to manage these things in a way that does not contaminate their hearts with agitation and anxiety.

In the Bible, rest is built on the foundation of trust in God, even in seemingly impossible circumstances. A great example of rest in the Bible is found in the psalms that David wrote during the years he ran from King Saul's murderous pursuit, particularly in Psalms 1–42. Despite being under intense and even deadly pressure, David continually sought God, trained himself to keep his focus on God, and, ultimately, trusted in God's protection, His provision, and, best of all, His presence. While this may seem counterintuitive, it *is* possible to rest in God during the most difficult times in our lives. Perhaps the only way that we can survive such difficult times is by making active decisions to rest in God. So, my friend, let's go a little deeper into this rest adventure to see where God leads us and what He will reveal!

What Is Rest?

I would say that rest is a state of being in which we maintain a peaceful heart, regardless of external pressures, situations, demands, or impossibilities. I like what Paul said to the Philippians: *"The peace of God, which surpasses all understanding, will guard your hearts and minds through Christ Jesus"* (Philippians 4:7). Based on this verse, I don't think it's possible to remain peaceful and experience rest without God's help.

Why We Don't Rest

How do we get ourselves into these places of unrest? If you think about it, rest has more to do with your lifestyle than your sleep quantity or the absence of stress. With this in mind, your lifestyle can get kind of crazy, even out of control, if you aren't careful. When you allow yourself to be put on impossible "hamster wheels" of activity, then your decisions have set you up to experience burn out, fatigue, and discouragement. You've allowed anxiety to settle into your heart at the expense of rest and peace. At this point, I'm preaching to the choir, because I'm often guilty of taking on too many things, getting in *way* over my head, and then drowning in everything. I do this to myself for lots of reasons. My biggest weak spots concerning rest come when I occasionally...

+ derive my sense of value and worth from achieving.

+ don't allow myself to be still and quiet, because I don't always like being around myself that much.

+ don't know how to rest, because it feels foreign, clumsy, awkward, irresponsible, lazy, and even downright uncomfortable.

+ get stuck in a frenzied pace, and I don't know how to get off the hamster wheel.

+ go through super busy seasons and neglect to scale back on my activities after it comes to an end.

+ get my priorities out of alignment, and my choices of how to spend my time become unhealthy, making rest the victim of my misaligned priorities.

+ confuse activity with accomplishment and fail to realize that just because I'm busy doesn't always mean that I'm accomplishing something—it just means I'm busy.

+ fail to rest out of pride, believing I'm some superwoman who can save the world from all its problems and dilemmas.

It is important to look at some of the reasons why we don't rest, because it helps us talk about the causes of our behaviors, not just the symptoms. Do any of the previous items sound familiar or hold an element of truth for you? Can you identify with any of those experiences? Do you have some other reasons why it becomes difficult for you to rest?

One of the things I really love about the Holy Spirit is that He leads me in truth. We know this because Jesus called Him the Spirit of truth (see John 16:13), and truth is extremely powerful. The reason the Spirit of truth is so powerful is because He leads us into the truth—the truth about the world in which we live, the truth about our actions and behaviors, and, perhaps most important, the truth about ourselves. So, as we think about rest, I'd encourage you to take a few minutes to pause and ask the Holy Spirit to reveal to you some deceptions you may have that prevent you from resting or making healthy choices on how to spend your time. Perhaps there are some things you have unknowingly allowed into your heart to poison the peace and rest that Jesus has for you. Allow the Holy Spirit to reveal these things to you, and be honest with yourself.

The Benefits of Rest

After taking some time to listen to the Holy Spirit speaking truth about our reasons for not resting, let's consider this important point: I think rest is like drinking water. When you're thirsty, you're already dehydrated. In the same way, when you're fatigued or feeling burnt out, you've probably already moved out of the rest zone and into fatigue for longer than you may realize. Moving out of rest and into anxiety and agitation can be a slippery slope, one that we can frequently go unnoticed, especially when we neglect to pay attention to the Holy Spirit.

Staying Functional

Rest helps us to function as healthy human beings, rather than sickly, dysfunctional, and fragmented ones. For example, when I was in college, there were a few semesters when I took on too many responsibilities, in addition to a full class load. At the end of these stressful semesters, I would come home entirely exhausted, broken, and barely able to function. Thankfully, my parents were supportive and would nurture me back to health with lots of rest, love, and care. Even though I'm well beyond college and the mistakes I've made there, I can still slip into the stress trap. And when I do, I tend to behave in dysfunctional and harmful ways, hurting both me and the people I love most—my family.

Creativity and Problem Solving

Another benefit of a lifestyle of rest is the ability to solve problems and be creative. When you think about this, it becomes painfully obvious that when we lack rest, our ability to think creatively and invent constructive solutions can get squeezed until it almost disappears. And the more complicated my life gets—managing multiple schedules, responsibilities, traveling, etc.—the more desperately I need to come up with creative ideas and solutions to problems. While I appreciate the fact that a certain amount of stress can help me to be productive, I also have to acknowledge that I'm not as effective as I can be when I don't incorporate rest into my lifestyle. If my family or friends read this, they'll probably fall off their chairs at that last sentence, but it's true, nevertheless. So if you find that you're struggling to solve problems or need more creativity in your life, please, take a minute to consider whether or not your lifestyle has a component of rest in it, on a healthy and consistent basis.

A Deeper Relationship with God

While I could give innumerable points related to the benefits of rest, let me conclude this section with what I consider to be the most important benefit of rest: a deeper relationship with God. There are many important responsibilities in our lives—family, work, school, relationships, church, and more—but I've found that when my relationship with God gets off-kilter, everything else tends to spiral into chaos. It's my sincere conviction that we all are uniquely designed to regularly connect in meaningful ways with our Creator, and that we have an intrinsic desire and hunger for fellowship with Him. Unfortunately, I think we are easily distracted and appeased with things that don't sustain nor fulfill.

In my own life, if I'm going to stay in a healthy and rested lifestyle, I need to be mindful of my daily routines and disciplines. For instance, the best time for me to have daily fellowship with God is in the morning, before my family gets up and before the day is in full gear. But I also readily admit that there are mornings when I'm tired and I'd prefer to sleep. Recently, I tried an experiment to see what would happen if I slept in one morning a week and skipped my prayer time with God. Needless to say, it was disastrous, and I only tried it twice. So, if I'm going to be consistent in my morning time with God, I have to be diligent to go to bed earlier the preceding night, which means I might miss something lame on TV! Of course, there are occasions when I stay up later, but they are the exception and not the rule. When I maintain this routine in my life, I tend to be more rested and settled in my heart, regardless of what's happening around me.

The Sabbath

Let me finish this section with some thoughts about a Jewish practice that seems to have been forgotten by many twenty-first-century Christians: the Sabbath. Sabbath is an interesting idea, and it originates in the creation narrative: *"And on the seventh day God ended His work which He had done, and He rested on the seventh day from all His work which He had done"* (Genesis 2:2). The practice of taking a day of rest became more formalized when God included the directive to keep the Sabbath holy in the Ten Commandments:

> *Remember the Sabbath day, to keep it holy. Six days you shall labor and do all your work, but the seventh day is the Sabbath of the LORD your God. In it you shall do no work: you, nor your son, nor your daughter, nor your male servant, nor your female servant, nor your cattle, nor your stranger who is within your gates. For in six days the LORD made the heavens and the earth, the sea, and all that is in them, and rested the seventh day. Therefore the LORD blessed the Sabbath day and hallowed it.* (Exodus 20:8–11)

To this day, practicing Jews continue to honor the Sabbath, setting aside a day of the week to pause from work, reflect, pray, and focus on their relationship with God. I have some Protestant friends who maintain a weekly Sabbath day. It is a time when they intentionally limit their activity and work events, being mindful to rest from life's busyness and focus more intently on God. I've given the idea of practicing a Sabbath a lot of thought and have considered whether or not our family could integrate it into our routine. As I'm writing this, I haven't yet figured out a way to do it, but I'm including the topic of Sabbath because it is highly relevant to the idea of rest and I think we would all do well to look into some ways that we could integrate it into our weekly routines. If you have some good ideas for how to do this within the context of a modern family schedule, I'd love to hear about it. Contact me on my Facebook page.

Components of Rest

As we conclude this chapter and move into some actual meditations on rest, let me give you a few finishing thoughts about the components of rest. Rest requires that we maintain healthy balance in our lives—a balance of work, school, exercise, sleep, diet, water intake, recreation, relationships, prayer, volunteering, time in Scripture, and even some general space and time to think and listen to God. To live a rested lifestyle is to be mindful of the responsibilities we take on and to make sure that we don't say yes to every good idea that comes along. When we make this mistake, we reduce our capacity to say "yes" to God's ideas, even sacrificing His will for our lives on the altar of good intentions.

Let me also throw in a monkey wrench into all of this. In my life, I've found that God opens doors of opportunity for me to serve and grow as a person that are *far* beyond my natural abilities, time considerations, and work capacity. In my natural thinking, I would automatically say no to these doors and opportunities, for fear of all the time, focus, and energy that they would require. At the same time, if I say yes to these chances, I know that I will have to trust God with greater dependence. For me, *the exercise of growing in my trust and dependence in God is part of the process of getting better at rest.* When I experience challenges that tax my abilities, my time management, and my work capacity, the best thing I can do is lean into God, admit my inadequacy, and trust Him, one minute at a time.

I say all of this with the premise that we do our absolute best, with the help of the Holy Spirit, to obey God and stay in sync with His directives—not running out in front of Him and not lagging behind. In Galatians 5:25, Paul encouraged us to stay in step with the Holy Spirit: *"If we live in the Spirit, let us also walk in the Spirit."* The idea behind Paul's direction is to maintain a type of military cadence with the pace and direction of the Holy Spirit, knowing full well that the Holy Spirit can lead us into situations that will require us to get better at trusting God and resting in His strength, wisdom, and power.

So, my friend, let's begin to meditate on what God has said about rest in His Word. As these words seep into your soul and spirit, allow them to change your thinking, priorities, and lifestyle, so that you can begin to lead a more rested and effective life!

7

MEDITATIONS ON REST

1. Rest When You Are Burdened

Though God says to come to Him when we are burdened, or "*heavy laden*" (Matthew 11:28), most of us are at war with ourselves, causing God to have to work the night shift.

Why do we battle within? I believe stress is a large portion of the problem. However, God did not intend for us to be stressed. The *Oxford Dictionary* describes stress as "a state of mental or emotional strain or tension resulting from adverse or very demanding circumstances." Stress originated in the garden of Eden when Adam and Eve disobeyed God's command. (See Genesis 3:17.) This insubordination separated them from a wonderful spiritual union with God. They sought leaves to swathe themselves and then hid when God called them. (See verse 8.) Why did they hide? Most likely it was because of the trauma of their wrongdoing. Before, they communed; now they wanted to be silent. Thankfully,

Jesus took away our curse and figuratively became a curse for us (see Deuteronomy 21:23, Galatians 3:13), that we might receive His rest.

I believe that if man had a choice, He would have asked God to make him before He made everything else, so that he could help God make creation. The reason I say this is that, currently, humanity keeps busy with his "nose to the grindstone," unable to relax. Even pleasure is marked with the challenge to have "fun." It's a work hard/play hard world. These pursuits leave many people "on edge." Contrast this way of living with the serene first days that Adam and Eve experienced in the garden.

The Bible says that the devil is restless. *"When an unclean spirit goes out of a man, he goes through dry places, seeking rest; and finding none, he says, 'I will return to my house from which I came'"* (Luke 11:24). God wants us to rest, even when we're burdened.

Scripture Memorization #1

"Come to Me, all you who labor and are heavy laden, and I will give you rest."
—Matthew 11:28

2. Rest on the Sabbath

Aren't Sundays wonderful? In the Old Testament, God gave His people a special day of the week in which to rest. *"Six days you shall labor and do all your work, but the seventh day is the Sabbath of the LORD your God. In it you shall do no work"* (Exodus 20:9–10). This is the longest commandment.

God not only wanted people to rest, but He also wanted the land to rest. *"Then the land shall enjoy its sabbaths as long as it lies desolate and you are in your enemies' land; then the land shall rest and enjoy its Sabbaths"* (Leviticus 26:34). For 490 years, the Israelites did not give the land the rest every seven years that God commanded. Eventually, God allowed Israel to be taken into captivity for seventy years, and the land had the respite it was owed. (490 divided by 7 equals 70!)

Adam and Eve's first full day on earth was the seventh day. Imagine, the creations of God walking in the garden of Eden without a care in the world, resting with their Father.

The walk of faith comes out of rest. In the Old Testament, the people of Israel were commanded to rest the last day of the week. They were probably exhausted and needed the respite. For the early church, the Sabbath was moved to the first day of the week. They rested in the resurrection power of the Holy Spirit as they started the week. Jesus arose on the first day of the week—what would become the Christian day of Sabbath. Jesus is the Lord of Sabbath.

When He walked the earth, Jesus performed most of His miracles on the Sabbath. By doing so, He discriminated between what man said and what God said. Remember what God told Adam and Eve? They didn't adhere to His command, but Jesus fulfilled God's commands even though it seemed that He was breaking Sabbath rules. He healed the man of dropsy (see Luke 14:1–6) and said to the Pharisees, who anxiously waited for Him to do wrong, *"Which of you, having a donkey or an ox that has fallen into a pit, will not immediately pull him out on the Sabbath day?"* (Luke 14:5).

Scripture Memorization #2

"And He said to them, 'The Sabbath was made for man, and not man for the Sabbath.'"
—Mark 2:27

3. Being at Rest

Let's look at what happened while Solomon was asleep.

"On that night God appeared to Solomon, and said to him, 'Ask what shall I give you?' And Solomon said to God....'Now give me wisdom and knowledge'" (2 Chronicles 1:7–8, 10).

I've taught this many times. Solomon asked for one of the most impressive things when he asked for wisdom. Buy why did he ask for that in particular?

Look at 1 Chronicles 22:12. It says, "Only may the LORD give you wisdom and understanding, and give you charge concerning Israel, that you may keep the law of the LORD your God." David prayed for God to give Solomon wisdom so that he could build the house of the Lord. He had also prepared many of the materials Solomon would need.

Solomon recalled that his father, David, told him that his way would be prosperous. The request for wisdom occurred after Solomon offered a thousand burnt offerings at Gibeon, within the tabernacle that Moses had made in the wilderness.

When we rest, God works. When we work, God rests. We can rest in our work. I proclaim every day to be a day of rest. I speak this early every morning. Sometimes I struggle to enter into this rest while I work. Sometimes I enter in, and then I fall out. I then fight to reenter that rest once again. However, I find that the struggle is worth it.

Scripture Memorization #3

"Let us therefore be diligent to enter that rest, lest anyone fall according to the same example of disobedience."
—Hebrews 4:11

4. Striving to Rest

Sleep is so important for everyone. If we neglect sleep, we take to a downhill path. God made us to have a certain amount of sleep every night.

Jehovah Rapha means "the Lord our Healer." The root of *Rapha* is rest. I have heard it said that all disease is caused from stress.

In John 5:17, Jesus said that both He and His Father "had been working." They worked on the Sabbath, and They work while we sleep. While we rest in Him, He is working.

Remember what happened when Jesus rested? He was asleep in the boat during a storm. How could He sleep at such a perilous time? On the shore, He told the disciples, *"Let us cross over to the other side of the lake"* (Luke 8:22). He spoke it because He knew they would make it.

However, several events took place between the time He spoke those words and when they got into the boat. Matthew records that a scribe approached Jesus and offered to follow Him. (See Matthew 8:19.) One of the disciples wanted to bury his father. (See verse 21.) Jesus conversed with both men but was determined to get to the other side, no matter what. He rested in His purpose.

Are we that determined in our pursuit of rest? When we learn that kind of determination, we, too, will be able to "loosen up" in the knowledge that we will get to the other side.

Trust in what He tells you and allow yourself to take a siesta in the boat.

Scripture Memorization #4

"It is vain for you to rise up early, to sit up late, to eat the bread of sorrows; for so He gives His beloved sleep."
—Psalm 127:2

5. The Sabbath Rest

God rested on the Sabbath, not because He was tired but because He was finished. On the cross, Jesus said, *"It is finished"* (John 19:30). The finished work of the cross and resurrection has made full provision for our rest and His work. After God rested, He *blessed* the Sabbath. (See Genesis 2:3.) We experience such blessing in our lives because He did that. Would we have rest in our lives if He hadn't done it? Would we have any relaxation, leisure, or sleep? There's restoration in rest.

The Lord's Prayer says, *"Give us this day our daily bread"* (Matthew 6:11). Jesus crossed the sea, walking on water. The disciples questioned Him about His arrival, noticing there was not another boat and knowing that He had not entered the boat with His disciples. Jesus' reply wasn't on the subject of His extraordinary mode of transportation but on their motives. (See John 6:25–26.) They sought food (bread), not miracles. He admonished them, *"Do not labor for the food which perishes, but for the food which endures to everlasting life"* (John 6:27).

They were full of questions, asking Him how they could begin to do the works of God. (See John 6:28.) *"Jesus answered and said to them, 'This is the work of God, that you believe in Him whom He sent'"* (verse 29). That is the bread of life. It seems so simple, but it is so challenging. Again, they asked for a sign, saying that their fathers had received bread from heaven. Once again, they were only seeking food for their bellies. Jesus said, *"I am the bread of life"* (John 6:35), and ended the exchange by saying, *"This is the will of Him who sent Me, that everyone who sees the Son and believes in Him may have everlasting life; and I will raise him up at the last day"* (verse 40). We can rest in His salvation.

Don't assume that everything depends on you. You are not a machine. Rest begins in your mind, and you can rest in His love. He calls us His beloved more than forty times in the New Testament. You are his beloved, and He says in Colossians 3:12, *"As the elect of God, holy and beloved, put on tender mercies, kindness, humility, meekness, longsuffering."*

Scripture Memorization #5

"Beloved, I pray that you may prosper in all things and be in health, just as your soul prospers."
—3 John 1–2

6. Heavenly Places

Are you a workaholic? If so, you need to rest.

But first, take a look at why you work so hard. Isn't it because you value work over any other activity? Why? A common reason is that workaholics don't feel good about themselves unless they are producing. They associate their self-worth with production. We need to take our eyes off our evaluation of ourselves and learn to accept what God has said about us: We are made in His image. (See Genesis 1:26.) What better credentials could we have?

Certainly, we cannot out do God, for even He, as the Son, rested. David, the psalmist, set his poetry to music. He sang in Psalm 110:1, "The LORD said to my Lord, 'Sit at My right hand, till I make Your enemies Your footstool.'" This is such an interesting psalm. It is quoted repeatedly in the New Testament. (See Luke 20:43; Hebrews 1:13; 10:13.) Jesus is revealed as seated in a position of rest in heaven. However, there are enemies on earth pitted against the gospel. If we're to be like Him, we can rest, too, even when we are battling foes.

Why is He seated? The reason is that *God is putting His enemies under His feet.*

Can you picture yourself seated with Jesus in heavenly places? The Bible says that's exactly what we do.

But God, who is rich in mercy, because of His great love with which He loved us, even when we were dead in trespasses, made us alive together with Christ (by grace you have been saved), and raised us up together, and made us sit together in the heavenly places in Christ Jesus.   (Ephesians 2:4–6)

We rest with Him in heavenly places.

Scripture Memorization #6

"For we are His workmanship, created in Christ Jesus for good works, which God prepared beforehand that we should walk in them."
—Ephesians 2:10

7. Rest and Renewal

Sometimes, you can feel "strung out"—with so many demands, so much furor swirling around you. Jesus and His disciples took time to rest. He said, "'*Come aside by yourselves to a deserted place and rest a while.' For there were many coming and going, and they did not even have time to eat*" (Mark 6:31). What did they need rest from?

The twelve apostles were sent out into every city, two by two. Seventy more followers were appointed to join them. (See Luke 10:1.) Jesus told them, "*The harvest truly is great, but the laborers are few; therefore pray the Lord of the harvest to send out laborers into His harvest*" (verse 2).

For their mission, they ventured out to heal the sick, cast out demons, and preach the kingdom of God, saying it "*has come near to you*" (verse 9).

You may say, "I don't go out and minister as they did. I don't need rest from all of that."

Do you have a job or a family to raise? Do you have a house to keep? Are you involved in volunteer programs? Do you pray for others? The everyday issues of life aren't likened to a "rat race" for no reason. Imagine those tiny mammals scurrying about on a wheel or careening through a maze in an attempt to escape. Our lives can mirror their antics, but they don't have to. I know I'd much rather listen to these wise words and not run myself silly: *"Come aside by yourselves"* (Mark 6:31).

Can you take divine direction?

Scripture Memorization #7

Come aside and rest...

"...and be renewed in the spirit of your mind."
—Ephesians 4:23

8. The Promised Rest

God promised His people a place to rest when He brought them out of Egypt. When they arrived at the Promised Land, Moses sent twelve spies into Canaan to check it out. Of the twelve spies, ten returned with a negative report. Only two, Joshua and Caleb, believed that God would help them to prevail no matter the obstacles. (See Numbers 13.) However, instead of resting on God's promises, the people believed the report of ten frightened spies. They refused to rest on God's Word but instead believed what the spineless emissaries reported.

We need to take great care that we heed the example given. In the book of Hebrews, it reiterates what happened in the wilderness.

Therefore, as the Holy Spirit says: "Today, if you will hear His voice, do not harden your hearts as in the rebellion, in the day of trial in the wilderness, where your fathers tested Me, tried Me, and saw My works forty years. Therefore I was angry with that generation, and said, 'They always go astray in their heart, and they have not known My ways.' So I swore in My wrath, 'They shall not enter My rest.'" (Hebrews 3:7–11)

The next verse says, "*Beware…*" (verse 12). This is like red and yellow flashing lights citing, "Danger! Danger!" What do we have to lose? The same thing the Israelites lost—rest. They faced days filled with doldrums, trekking through the desert to the Promised Land. Is that how we want to live?

Kadesh Barnea is a city on the border of Canaan. It was such a short distance away, but yet so far, because they did not rest on God's promises. Because of the Israelites' disobedience and lack of faith, they would not enter the Promised Land. *Only* the next generation would go in with Joshua and Caleb.

Joshua and Caleb remained as young as the generation that entered with them. When you rest on God's Word, you not only receive His promise, but He also renews you, allowing a youthful you to enter the Promised Land.

Scripture Memorization #8

"For all the promises of God in Him are Yes, and in Him Amen, to the glory of God through us."
—2 Corinthians 1:20

9. Rest and Seeking

Seven is the number of perfection. Do you think God chose to relax on the seventh day for no reason? Rest brings restoration and completion, but it has to be sought.

Jesus yearned for rest. Even though He never rushed when he walked the earth, taking things in stride, He wasn't ruffled, even when people wanted to kill Him. He said, *"My Father has been working until now, and I have been working"* (John 5:17).

These days, there seems to be a "hurry disease." We don't know how to rest, especially when we are in difficult circumstances. We don't know how to relax.

The Israelites sought a resting place. *"So they departed from the mountain of the LORD on a journey of three days; and the ark of the covenant of the LORD went before them for the three days' journey, to search out a resting place for them"* (Numbers 10:33). The *New American Standard Bible* translates *"search out"* as *"seek out."* In each version, we see that rest requires resolve.

When the Israelites were in the wilderness, they looked to a bronze statue of a serpent for healing from snake bites. (See Numbers 21:9.) All they did was look at it, and they were healed. Today, we look to Jesus. When we look to Him, we receive healing from our "hurry disease."

The Israelites sought a land in which to rest with the ark. We will find rest as we pursue *"things which are above"* (Colossians 3:1). What's above us?

Look to Jesus.

Scripture Memorization #9

"If then you were raised with Christ, seek those things which are above, where Christ is, sitting at the right hand of God."
—Colossians 3:1

10. Receiving His Best with a Mind on Rest

God has an interesting way of speaking to us when we are resting.

There are thirty-four dreams recorded in the Bible.

In Genesis, Joseph's life was completely driven by dreams. He was seventeen when God first spoke to him in dreams. Through those dreams, God revealed to him that He would save his family, making possible the eventual covenant family that would bring forth the Messiah.

Joseph's dreams also saved the land of Egypt, when he interpreted the dreams of the pharaoh, enabling them to avoid a coming famine, and securing Joseph's place as second in command of Egypt.

I'm looking forward to peace, once more, between Egypt and Israel. As the Bible says,

> In that day there will be a highway from Egypt to Assyria, and the Assyrian will come into Egypt and the Egyptian into Assyria, and the Egyptians will serve with the Assyrians. In that day Israel will be one of three with Egypt and Assyria; a blessing in the midst of the land, whom the LORD of hosts shall bless, saying, "Blessed is Egypt My people, and Assyria the work of My hands, and Israel My inheritance."
>
> (Isaiah 19:23–25)

The Joseph of the New Testament took Mary and Jesus to Egypt, and he knew when to return and where to return to. (See Matthew 2.)

God speaks to us when we rest and tune in to Him. Certainly, not every dream is from God. But I have found that He speaks to my spirit when I rest.

Scripture Memorization #10

"When you roam, they will lead you; when you sleep, they will keep you; and when you awake, they will speak with you."
—Proverbs 6:22

11. Rest at the Well

Live right, from the inside out. When you try to save yourself, you take in vain Christ's death. Jesus gave His greatest revelation of Himself to the woman at the well (see John 4) and the blind man (see John 9). Both were surprised by His love and miracle-working power.

Jesus went through Samaria (or Shomron), a mountainous region in northern Palestine. Samaria was once the capital of the Kingdom of Israel, before they were conquered by the Assyrians.

Talk spread about His disciples, who baptized and made disciples; so He headed back to Galilee. He came to Sychar (now called Askar), a plot of ground Jacob gave to his son Joseph. This is the place where Joseph's bones were buried hundreds of years after they were carried from Egypt. (I love how the Old Testament weaves exquisitely into the New.) This was also the location of Jacob's well.

The Samaritan woman came to the water supply, and Jesus asked her for a drink. When she expressed shock that He would ask her for such a thing, Jesus said, *"If you knew the gift of God, and who it is who says to you, 'Give Me a drink,' you would have asked Him, and He would have given you living water"* (John 4:10). She then asked Jesus if He was greater than her ancestor Jacob, who gave them the well.

The Samaritan woman found her rest in Jesus at the well. She had six men in her life, and Jesus was the seventh, her Sabbath. Likewise, the blind man was healed, both outside and inside, on the Sabbath. (See John 9:1–14.)

Scripture Memorization #11

"And since we have the same spirit of faith, according to what is written, 'I believed and therefore I spoke.'"
—2 Corinthians 4:13

12. Rest with Your Tongue

Resting in Jesus each day is a goal that can be attained. One of the ways I have achieved this, ever since I was twenty-three years old, is by praying in the Holy Spirit.

I began reading the Bible when I was ten years old. I even began to memorize certain Scriptures. However, when I received Jesus as my Savior at the age of sixteen, the author of the Bible came into my heart, and I was "hooked on the Book." By age twenty-three, I had received the baptism of the Holy Spirit.

Jesus promised this baptism before He ascended.

And being assembled together with them, He commanded them not to depart from Jerusalem, but to wait for the Promise of the Father, "which," He said, "you have heard from Me; for John truly baptized with water, but you shall be baptized with the Holy Spirit not many days from now."

(Acts 1:4–5)

As recorded in the book of John, Jesus told them that though He was leaving them, He would send a Comforter—the Holy Spirit. John the Baptist spoke of this also when he said, "*I indeed baptize you with water; but One mightier than I is coming, whose sandal strap I am not worthy to loose. He will baptize you with the Holy Spirit and fire*" (Luke 3:16).

When I pray in my prayer language, it goes beyond my under-standing. Many times, I *rest* as I drive to work, letting the Spirit pray over the needs and problems—both those I recognize and those I do not—because the Spirit gives the utterance. (See Acts 2:4.)

Scripture Memorization #12

"To whom He said, 'This is the rest with which
You may cause the weary to rest,' and, 'This is the refreshing';
yet they would not hear."
—Isaiah 28:12

13. Rest When You're Barren

"He grants the barren woman a home, like a joyful mother of children. Praise the LORD!"
—Psalm 113:9

Our rest was purchased at the cross. *"But He was wounded for our transgressions, He was bruised for our iniquities; the chastisement for our peace was upon Him, and by His stripes we are healed"* (Isaiah 53:5). In Isaiah 54:1, He tells the barren to sing. Then He tells them to get ready for an incredible blessing—a blessing that *will* affect the entire earth. (See verses 2–3.)

When Wally and I started our church more than fifty years ago, we began with twenty-two people. A prophet proclaimed Isaiah 54:2–3 over our ministry. He said,

Enlarge the place of your tent, and let them stretch out the curtains of your dwellings; do not spare; lengthen your cords, and strengthen your stakes. For you shall expand to the right and to the left, and your descendants will inherit the nations, and make the desolate cities inhabited.

He said there would always be two camps. The church became the *"stakes"* we were to strengthen, and the media outreach became the *"cords"* we were to lengthen.

My husband has always had a worship ministry. We were barren, but he sang. We became known as "Happy Church." Today, our reach stretches all around the world. Do you feel barren? Sing!

Scripture Memorization #13

"'Sing, O barren, you who have not borne! Break forth into singing, and cry aloud, you who have not labored with child! For more are the children of the desolate than the children of the married woman,' says the Lord."
—Isaiah 54:1

14. Rest from Your Work

God said, *"Sit at My right hand, till I make Your enemies Your footstool"* (Psalm 110:1). In Hebrews, we read, *"But this Man [Jesus], after He had offered one sacrifice for sins forever, sat down at the right hand of God, from that time waiting till His enemies are made His footstool"* (Hebrews 10:12–13). For Jesus, this was a position of rest. After completing His work on the cross, He now rests at the right hand of God, while His enemies serve as His footstool.

Who were the enemies of Jesus, and aren't they our enemies also?

The first we think about are the Pharisees. They didn't want Jesus to heal or preach. Do we have pharisaical tendencies in our lives? Then there is the carnal nature as mentioned in Romans 8:7: *"The carnal mind is enmity [hostile] against God."* I'm sure many of us can confirm its presence in our lives. We can verify these and many more enemies of Christ, but when we are saved, then we are in Christ. We are seated next to Christ, resting in Him, while God makes our enemies our footstool.

Scripture Memorization #14

"…and raised us up together, and made us sit together in the heavenly places in Christ Jesus."
—Ephesians 2:6

15. Rest in the Midst of Turmoil

We live in a hyperactive world.

> [The angel of the LORD] *said, "Go out, and stand on the*
> *mountain before the LORD." And behold, the LORD passed*
> *by, and a great and strong wind tore into the mountains and*
> *broke the rocks in pieces before the LORD, but the LORD was*
> *not in the wind; and after the wind an earthquake, but the*
> *LORD was not in the earthquake; and after the earthquake a*
> *fire, but the LORD was not in the fire; and after the fire a still*
> *small voice. So it was, when Elijah heard it, that he wrapped*
> *his face in his mantle and went out and stood in the entrance*
> *of the cave. Suddenly a voice came to him, and said, "What*
> *are you doing here, Elijah?"*   (1 Kings 19:11–13)

How can we hear God's voice among so many other voices?
We can do it by finding a place of peace in which to hear His voice.
Should we do this in the car, the bathroom, or the basement?
Elijah found that when he wrapped his face in his mantle, or outer
cloak, he found a place of peace and was able to hear the still, small
voice of God.

Do you think you have problems? A "hit" was put upon Elijah's
life. Jezebel vowed to kill him in revenge for the prophets who had
been killed. As a result, Elijah fled.

When we're fleeing from turmoil, we, too, can "wrap our face in our mantle."

Do you want to find a place of rest in your heart? Stop and listen! After Elijah listened, he was no longer depressed! The enemy will give you vain imaginations of fear and turmoil, but, like Elijah, you can receive peace in your heart! Elijah's circumstances didn't change, and neither will yours! Rest in God, and He will give you a hearing ear!

Scripture Memorization #15

"You will keep him in perfect peace, whose mind is stayed on You, because he trusts in You."
—Isaiah 26:3

16. Rest in His Care

Job 10:12 says, *"You have granted me life and favor, and Your care has preserved my spirit."* The Lord's visitation is to preserve us. We don't want to miss His visit.

Sometimes I think He chooses the strangest modes of intervention. It can be in a dream, because we are resting. God visited Nebuchadnezzar in a dream when he was resting! (See Daniel 2.) God visits sinners and saints in dreams. Sometimes you can be in the middle of a discussion when He visits you with a small word that gives you just the right bit of wisdom for your situation. And just recently, Sarah had a confrontation with an angry woman, and God dropped a word in her heart, which miraculously settled the situation.

Why do we receive these deliverances? Because He cares for us.

Psalm 91:2, 4 says, *"I will say of the Lord, 'He is my refuge and my fortress; my God, in Him I will trust.'....He shall cover you with His feathers, and under His wings you shall take refuge; His truth shall be your shield and buckler."* What a wonderful promise! We can rest in His protection!

Jesus told His disciples, *"Are not two sparrows sold for a copper coin? And not one of them falls to the ground apart from your Father's will. But the very hairs of your head are all numbered.*

Do not fear therefore; you are of more value than many sparrows" (Matthew 10:29–31). A sparrow was sold for very little in those days and was considered most insignificant. So we can rest in the knowledge that we are of more value than the lowest.

Scripture Memorization #16

"Rest in the LORD, and wait patiently for Him; do not fret because of him who prospers in his way, because of the man who brings wicked schemes to pass."
—Psalm 37:7

17. Rest from Worry

When we run into problems, we usually fret. When we hear bad news, we fall apart. Sometimes, what we fret about is not even true, but we don't check facts before worrying.

When God called me into the ministry, it was not common for women to preach. And it was not easily accepted. Plus, there was the fact that I was forty-two years old! However, I have found that God is not concerned about age, color, or gender. He is looking for faith! Stay in His Word! In the midst of it all, He will keep you on course!

Scripture Memorization #17

"For thus says the Lord GOD, the Holy One of Israel: 'In returning and rest you shall be saved; in quietness and confidence shall be your strength.'"
—Isaiah 30:15

18. Rest in the Midst of Loss

There are fourteen seasons in the book of Ecclesiastes. They are contrasting seasons in our lives.

In my life, I especially enjoyed the season of raising children. That season was busy and challenging but extremely fulfilling. I enjoyed going to my children's activities, such as baseball and basketball games. And getting them ready for proms was delightful.

But there comes the season when it is time for our children to leave home, and we become empty nesters. Like many changes, this calls for flexibility. And perhaps there is nothing that makes the nest feel emptier than when we lose a mate!

I have found this Scripture brings light in every season.

Scripture Memorization #18

"He has made everything beautiful in its time. Also He has put eternity in their hearts."
—Ecclesiastes 3:11

19. Rest When You Are Tired

Sometimes we feel so exhausted we just want to drop out.

The first time I went to Russia was right after the Iron Curtain fell. We wanted to hold healing meetings in Moscow and Kiev, and there was a lot of confusion in the process. When we finally reached Kiev, we had been traveling for twenty-two hours. I was exhausted! Upon our arrival, we were met by some students from Oral Roberts University, who were to transport us to our hotel. They had other plans, however.

They said, "We would like to take you somewhere else and have you pray for a demon-possessed girl."

I silently spoke to God, saying, "I am so tired, God!"

And I remember so clearly His response. He said, "I'm not!"

He gave me His rest! And the girl was wonderfully delivered, and she received Jesus as her Savior! Receive His rest when you are tired!

Scripture Memorization #19

"Who satisfies your mouth with good things, so that your youth is renewed like the eagle's."
—Psalm 103:5

20. Rest When You Need Faith

When you have Jesus, you have everything!

When I was starting on television forty-four years ago, I went to be interviewed by a secular board of nine men. They said, "You have no religious education and you really do not have a presence for television. Stay with radio." One man interrupted and said, "Let's try her. I believe she will pay her bills."

Reluctantly, the others agreed. None of those men are still in the television industry. Interestingly, I still am!

Scripture Memorization #20

"For assuredly, I say to you, whoever says to this mountain, 'Be removed and be cast into the sea,' and does not doubt in his heart, but believes that those things he says will be done, he will have whatever he says."
—Mark 11:23

21. Rest in Your Identity in Christ

The greatest rest we can receive is when we see who we are in Jesus Christ.

We have an adopted son who is now fifty-three years old. He had some challenges with drugs and alcohol in his teen years. Then, a wonderful man in our church convinced him to go to a rehab center. It was a great blessing to him because he was really freed of both addictions.

When I would think about my son, I would often condemn myself and then repent, many times over. Finally, God spoke to me and said, *When you repented the first time, I forgave you. You have My righteousness.*

Such peace came into my heart!

Scripture Memorization #21

"If Christ is in you, the body is dead because of sin, but the Spirit is life because of righteousness."
—Romans 8:10

22. Rest When You Are in Danger

God has opened unusual doors for me in Muslim countries. When I go there, Jesus heals the sick, and Muslims actually believe these miracles because the Koran testifies Jesus' healing power. They come to our healing meetings by the thousands. Not only do they receive Jesus as their Healer, but they also receive Him as their Savior.

I've been to Pakistan six times. During one visit, thirty-four suicide bombers made a pact to kill me and blow up the stadium where we hosted our healing meetings. We had to move the meeting to another venue but still had marvelous results. Every night, when I stood on the platform to minister, I knew there was a possibility that I could be shot. However, I had great peace and rest! How I filled my mind with Hebrews 13:5!

Scripture Memorization #22

"For [Jesus] *Himself has said,*
'I will never leave you nor forsake you.'"
—Hebrews 13:5

23. Rest When You Need to Be Loved

When my husband thought I was discouraged, he would say to me, "Marilyn, what you need is some TLC!"

What is TLC? It is tender loving care!

My husband would do special things for me. Our marriage was a very sweet time in my life! However, he has since gone to heaven. But I still enjoy much TLC! You can, also.

Scripture Memorization #23

"The LORD has appeared of old to me, saying: 'Yes, I have loved you with an everlasting love; therefore with lovingkindness I have drawn you.'"
—Jeremiah 31:3

24. Rest in Challenging Times

We live in a world filled with violence and fear. Thirty minutes of watching the nightly newscasts can overwhelm you in anxiety and fear! How can we rest in such bad circumstances?

Several years ago, I ministered at a church growth conference in Japan. It was a very fruitful time. The results were awesome!

On the final night after the last service, I returned to my hotel room exhausted. And when sleeping, I had the worst nightmare I have ever had. It was concerning Sarah, who was studying in Germany at the time. I jumped out of bed and began to pray!

Later, I learned how actively the enemy was attacking her. Thank God, He brought her through!

Here is a special Scripture to uphold you in challenging times.

Scripture Memorization #24

"Also, the descendants of His servants shall inherit it, and those who love His name shall dwell in it."
—Psalm 59:36

25. Rest in the Joy of the Lord

We all enjoy experiencing special times with family, friends, and good food in a nice environment! That is why we often look forward to the holidays. But do we realize that the joy of the Lord is available to us at all times?

Some time ago, I was ministering in El Salvador with some others, and we were driving to a remote area in the country. It was hot and humid, and there was no air-conditioning in the car. Along the route, we stopped at a stand to buy some mangoes. I will never forget how the joy of the Lord enfolded us as we climbed out of the car to get a treat on that hot day in the jungle!

Just as we experienced that day, we can all have a party with the Lord all of the time! Rest in His joy!

Scripture Memorization #25

"But he who is of a merry heart has a continual feast."
—Proverbs 15:15

26. Rest in God's Power

Prior to Pentecost, Peter was an "I-and-they" man. He was full of confidence that even if they (the other disciples) would fail, he would prevail. Just before Jesus predicted Peter's forthcoming denial, the disciple proclaimed, "*Even if all are made to stumble because of You, I will never be made to stumble*" (Matthew 26:33). Peter was depending on his own power, and his failure would be complete.

After receiving the power of the Holy Spirit, however, Peter said, "*We cannot but speak the things which we have seen and heard*" (Acts 4:20). The disciples had been filled with fear before Pentecost, but now, they were filled with spiritual power.

Likewise, you have great rest within when you surrender to His power.

Scripture Memorization #26

"If you then, being evil, know how to give good gifts to your children, how much more will your heavenly Father give the Holy Spirit to those who ask Him!"
—Luke 11:13

27. Rest in God's Wisdom

At times, I feel as though my mind is like a scrambled egg when it came to making decisions! Which way should I go? What should I do?

When Wally and I started in the ministry, we were assistant pastors at a church in Amarillo, Texas. I was very discontent with the apartment the church had provided. I constantly nagged Wally to threaten the senior pastor that we would quit if they did not provide better living arrangements.

When Wally refused to do so, I said, "I am going to my mother's in Denver."

This did not move him, either. So I left for Denver on a train.

On the way, God gave me a Scripture I did not want to hear. Revelation 3:8 says, "*I have set before you an open door, and no one can shut it.*" Then, when I arrived in Denver, a friend called and gave me the same Scripture verse. I returned to Amarillo, and that is when I first began to teach the Bible.

We can rest in God's wisdom!

Scripture Memorization #27

"Wisdom is the principal thing; therefore get wisdom. And in all your getting, get understanding."
—1 Corinthians 6:20

28. Rest in God's Direction

Sometimes, we need to rest, be still, and hear God's Word in our inner man.

Take time to listen for God. We need to constantly feed on His Word! When His Word is inside us, He can bring a personal word to us. This personal word is called a *rhema*.

Several years ago, I had an invitation to go to a large Muslim country to minister. I immediately wanted to say yes! However, when I began to pray about it, God spoke to me. He said, *Where I lead you, I will protect you. I am not leading you there.*

I chose not to go and rested in His wisdom.

Scripture Memorization #28

"If you abide in Me, and My words abide in you, you will ask what you desire, and it shall be done for you."
—John 15:7

29. Rest in a Calm Spirit

There are times when we open our mouths without knowledge. Sometimes, we need to have a calm spirit.

I had a relative who became jealous whenever a female coworker began speaking to her husband. She was about to confront the woman when she found out that the coworker was helping her husband select a birthday gift for her.

In this verse, Solomon advised us to have a calm spirit and a warm heart. May we heed his advice!

Scripture Memorization #29

"He who has knowledge spares his words, and a man of understanding is of a calm spirit."
—Proverbs 17:27

30. Rest in Surrender to God's Will

The greatest peace comes from surrendering to God, but surrendering to God's will can be challenging. When I was studying at the university to get my degree in foreign languages, I thought I was in love. But there were issues in which we did not agree.

My mother was a great woman of prayer. She prayed that I would surrender to God and His will in choosing a life mate. In my heart, I knew the issues we did not agree on were spiritual values.

When I surrendered to God's will, He assured me that I could trust Him for a mate. In that act of surrender, I found peace.

Scripture Memorization #30

"For all the promises of God in Him are Yes, and in Him Amen, to the glory of God through us."
—2 Corinthians 1:20

ABOUT THE AUTHORS

Marilyn Hickey

As founder and president of Marilyn Hickey Ministries, Marilyn is being used by God to help cover the earth with the Word. Her Bible teaching ministry is an international outreach via television, satellite, books, CDs, DVDs, and healing meetings. Marilyn has established an international program of Bible and food distribution, and she is committed to overseas ministry, often bringing the gospel to people who have never heard it before.

Marilyn's message of encouragement to all believers emphasizes the fact that today can be the best day of your life if Jesus Christ is living in you.

Marilyn, along with her late husband, Wallace Hickey, founded the Orchard Road Christian Center in Greenwood Village, Colorado. She has two grown children, five grandchildren, and four great-grandchildren.

Sarah Bowling

Sarah Bowling, the daughter of Marilyn Hickey, is vice president of Marilyn Hickey Ministries and cohost of the internationally broadcast television program *Today with Marilyn and Sarah*. She is the founder of Saving Moses, a humanitarian initiative dedicated to reducing infant mortality throughout the world. She is also a guest speaker at seminars, conferences, and college campuses worldwide. Sarah and her husband, Reece, are senior pastors of Orchard Road Christian Center. They have three children and live in the Denver area.

Meditation #1

"Come to Me, all you who labor and are heavy laden, and I will give you rest."
—Matthew 11:28

Meditation #2

"And He said to them, 'The Sabbath was made for man, and not man for the Sabbath.'"
—Mark 2:27

Meditation #3

"Let us therefore be diligent to enter that rest, lest anyone fall according to the same example of disobedience."
—Hebrews 4:11

Meditation #4

"It is vain for you to rise up early, to sit up late, to eat the bread of sorrows; for so He gives His beloved sleep."
—Psalm 127:2

Meditation #5

"Beloved, I pray that you may prosper in all things and be in health, just as your soul prospers."
—3 John 1–2

Rest When You Are Burdened

Why do we battle within? I believe stress is a large
portion of the problem. However, God did not intend for
us to be stressed.

Rest on the Sabbath

Adam and Eve's first full day on earth was the seventh day.
Imagine, the creations of God walking in the garden of
Eden without a care in the world, resting with their Father.

Being at Rest

When we rest, God works. When we work,
God rests. We can rest in our work.
I proclaim every day to be a day of rest.

Striving to Rest

Sleep is so important for everyone. If we neglect sleep, we
take to a downhill path. God made us to have a certain
amount of sleep every night.

The Sabbath Rest

Don't assume that everything depends on you.
You are not a machine. Rest begins in your mind,
and you can rest in God's love.

Meditation #6

"For we are His workmanship, created in Christ Jesus for good works, which God prepared beforehand that we should walk in them."
—Ephesians 2:10

Meditation #7

"...and be renewed in the spirit of your mind."
—Ephesians 4:23

Meditation #8

"For all the promises of God in Him are Yes, and in Him Amen, to the glory of God through us."
—2 Corinthians 1:20

Meditation #9

"If then you were raised with Christ, seek those things which are above, where Christ is, sitting at the right hand of God."
—Colossians 3:1

Meditation #10

"When you roam, they will lead you; when you sleep, they will keep you; and when you awake, they will speak with you."
—Proverbs 6:22

Heavenly Places

We need to take our eyes off our evaluation of ourselves
and learn to accept what God has said about us: We are
made in His image. What better credentials could we have?

Rest and Renewal

Sometimes, you can feel "strung out"—with so many
demands, so much furor swirling around you. Jesus and
His disciples took time to rest.

The Promised Rest

When you rest on God's Word, you not only receive His
promise, but He also renews you, allowing a youthful you
to enter the Promised Land.

Rest and Seeking

Rest brings restoration and completion,
but it has to be sought.

Receiving His Best with a Mind on Rest

God speaks to us when we rest and tune in to Him.

Meditation #11

*"And since we have the same spirit of faith, according to what
is written, 'I believed and therefore I spoke.'"*
—2 Corinthians 4:13

Meditation #12

*"To whom He said, 'This is the rest with which
You may cause the weary to rest,' and,
'This is the refreshing'; yet they would not hear."*
—Isaiah 28:12

Meditation #13

*"'Sing, O barren, you who have not borne! Break forth into
singing, and cry aloud, you who have not labored with child!
For more are the children of the desolate than the children of
the married woman,' says the LORD."*
—Isaiah 54:1

Meditation #14

*"...and raised us up together, and made us sit together in the
heavenly places in Christ Jesus."*
—Ephesians 2:6

Meditation #15

*"You will keep him in perfect peace, whose mind is stayed on
You, because he trusts in You."*
—Isaiah 26:3

Rest at the Well

Live right, from the inside out. When you try to save yourself, you take in vain Christ's death.

Rest with Your Tongue

Resting in Jesus each day is a goal that can be attained. One of the ways I have achieved this, ever since I was twenty-three years old, is by praying in the Holy Spirit.

Rest When You're Barren

In Isaiah 54:1, God tells the barren to sing. Then He tells them to get ready for an incredible blessing—a blessing that will affect the entire earth.

Rest from Your Work

We are seated next to Christ, resting in Him, while God makes our enemies our footstool.

Rest in the Midst of Turmoil

How can we hear God's voice among so many other voices? We can do it by finding a place of peace in which to hear his voice.

Meditation #16

"Rest in the Lord, *and wait patiently for Him; do not fret because of him who prospers in his way, because of the man who brings wicked schemes to pass."*
—Psalm 37:7

Meditation #17

"For thus says the Lord God, *the Holy One of Israel: 'In returning and rest you shall be saved; in quietness and confidence shall be your strength.'"*
—Isaiah 30:15

Meditation #18

"He has made everything beautiful in its time. Also He has put eternity in their hearts."
—Ecclesiastes 3:11

Meditation #19

"Who satisfies your mouth with good things, so that your youth is renewed like the eagle's."
—Psalm 103:5

Meditation #20

"For assuredly, I say to you, whoever says to this mountain, 'Be removed and be cast into the sea,' and does not doubt in his heart, but believes that those things he says will be done, he will have whatever he says."
—Mark 11:23

Rest in His Care

Sometimes you can be in the middle of a discussion when He visits you with a small word that gives you just the right bit of wisdom for your situation.

Rest from Worry

I have found that God is not concerned about age, color, or gender. He is looking for faith! Stay in His Word!

Rest in the Midst of Loss

But there comes the season when it is time for our children to leave home, and we become empty nesters. Like many changes, this calls for flexibility.

Rest When You Are Tired

Sometimes we feel so exhausted we just want to drop out. Receive His rest when you are tired!

Rest When You Need Faith

When you have Jesus, you have everything!

Meditation #21

"If Christ is in you, the body is dead because of sin, but the Spirit is life because of righteousness."
—Romans 8:10

Meditation #22

*"For [Jesus] Himself has said,
'I will never leave you nor forsake you.'"*
—Hebrews 13:5

Meditation #23

"The LORD has appeared of old to me, saying: 'Yes, I have loved you with an everlasting love; therefore with lovingkindness I have drawn you.'"
—Jeremiah 31:3

Meditation #24

"Also, the descendants of His servants shall inherit it, and those who love His name shall dwell in it."
—Psalm 59:36

Meditation #25

"But he who is of a merry heart has a continual feast."
—Proverbs 15:15

Rest in Your Identity in Christ

The greatest rest we can receive is when we see who we are in Jesus Christ.

Rest When You Are in Danger

God has opened unusual doors for me in Muslim countries….Every night, when I stood on the platform to minister, I knew there was a possibility that I could be shot. However, I had great peace and rest!

Rest When You Need to Be Loved

What is TLC? It is tender loving care!… I still enjoy much TLC! You can, also.

Rest in Challenging Times

We live in a world filled with violence and fear. Thirty minutes of watching the nightly newscasts can overwhelm you in anxiety and fear! Here is a special Scripture to uphold you in challenging times.

Rest in the Joy of the Lord

We all enjoy experiencing special times with family, friends, and good food in a nice environment! That is why we often look forward to the holidays. But do we realize that the joy of the Lord is available to us at all times?

Meditation #26

"If you then, being evil, know how to give good gifts to your children, how much more will your heavenly Father give the Holy Spirit to those who ask Him!"
—Luke 11:13

Meditation #27

"Wisdom is the principal thing; therefore get wisdom. And in all your getting, get understanding."
—1 Corinthians 6:20

Meditation #28

"If you abide in Me, and My words abide in you, you will ask what you desire, and it shall be done for you."
—John 15:7

Meditation #29

"He who has knowledge spares his words, and a man of understanding is of a calm spirit."
—Proverbs 17:27

Meditation #30

"For all the promises of God in Him are Yes, and in Him Amen, to the glory of God through us."
—2 Corinthians 1:20

Rest in God's Power

You have great rest within when
you surrender to His power.

Rest in God's Wisdom

At times, I feel as though my mind is like a scrambled egg
when it came to making decisions! Which way should I
go? What should I do? We can rest in God's wisdom!

Rest in God's Direction

Sometimes, we need to rest, be still, and hear God's
Word in our inner man. Take time to listen for God.

Rest in a Calm Spirit

There are times when we open our mouths without
knowledge. Sometimes, we need to have a calm spirit.

Rest in Surrender to God's Will

When I surrendered to God's will, He assured me that
I could trust Him for a mate. In that act of surrender, I
found peace.